d • AK-48 • American Dre[...]un
ans Haze #3 • Aurora [...]52
Tooth • Big Bang • Big Buddha Cheese
h Haze • Burmese Kush • Casey Jones
D-Line • Ed Rosenthal Super Bud • F-13
• G-13 Diesel • Gonzo #1 • Grandaddy
Hash Heaven • Haze Mist • Ice Cream
ean • Kaya • KC-36 • KC-45 • Kish
owryder #2 • Mako Haze • Martian Mean
Mount Cook • Nuken • Opium • Posh
Sour Cream • (IBL) Sour Diesel • Speed
s) Strawberry Haze • Sweet 105 • The
e Third Dimension • TNR • True Blue
Haze #2 • Venus • Very Berry Haze
e Rhino • White Satin • Wonder Woman

The Big Book of BUDS

volume 3

The Big Book of BUDS

More Marijuana Varieties from the World's Great Seed Breeders

Edited by Ed Rosenthal

Quick American

The Big Book of Buds Volume 3
Copyright 2007 Quick Trading Company

Photographs in The Big Book of Buds Volume 3 appear courtesy of the contributors, photo credits belong to company unless otherwise indicated.

Published by Quick American
A division of Quick Trading Company
Oakland, California
ISBN-10: 0-932551-82-3
ISBN-13: 978-0-932551-82-5

Executive Editor: Ed Rosenthal
Project Editor: S. Newhart
Photo Coordinator: Hera Lee
Cover and Interior Design: Scott Idleman/Blink
Cover photo: Subcool

Printed in China.

Variety descriptions and breeder stories compiled by S. Newhart with the assistance of John Carnahan.

We wish to thank all Big Book of Buds 3 contributors for providing articles, information and photos. Without your participation and support, this project would not have been possible.

Publisher's Cataloging-in-Publication
(Provided by Quality Books, Inc.)

The Big Book of Buds. Volume 3, More marijuana varieties
    From the world's great seed breeders / edited by Ed
Rosenthal.
        p. cm.
        Includes index.
        ISBN-13: 978-0-932551-79-5
        ISBN-10: 0-932551-79-3
        ISBN-13: 978-0-932551-82-5
        ISBN-10: 0-932551-82-3

        1. Marijuana. 2. Cannabis.   I. Rosenthal, Ed.

    SB295.C35B542 2007   633.7'9
                                  QBI07-600037

This book is dedicated to Raphael Mechoulam,
the grandfather of modern cannabis research.

It seldom turns out the way
it does in the song
Once in a while
you get shown the light
in the strangest of places
if you look at it right

From "Scarlet Begonias"—
words by Robert Hunter, music by Jerry Garcia
("Scarlet Begonias" composed and written by Jerry Garcia
and Robert Hunter. Reproduced by arrangement with
Ice Nine Publishing Co., Inc. (ASCAP)

Contents

Introduction

By Ed Rosenthal

Big Book of Buds 3 is witness to a new generation of marijuana strains. With thousands of crosses, inbred strains and hybrids already available, one might ask what more is there to perfect? Why bother with more breeding?

The new plants described in this book answer these questions. These plants are the result of third and fourth wave breeding. They are far advanced from the older varieties that were developed 10 or 20 years ago. They are faster growing, higher yielding, more adapted to thrive in particular environments and, most importantly, they produce better highs.

Improvements have themselves been subject to evolution. Every breeder has a different set of visions and goals. They breed toward these goals to create unique varieties. These improvements are in turn incorporated, and often supplemented, by other breeders, resulting in new strains.

The first breeding wave, which is now called old school, consisted of adapted landraces. These were pure strains or simple crosses that modified the plants just enough to allow them to be grown indoors or to ripen outdoors. This was typified by "90-day wonders" which were a major improvement over unmodified stash seeds. Afghani-Mexican and other simple sativa-indica crosses are typical of the era.

The second wave was based on hybridization of strains with the three goals of increasing potency and yield while decreasing flowering time. For the first time, the major breeding emphasis was devoted to indoor crops. Domesticated strains were crossed with each other, and new exotic lines from Africa, Brazil, and India were introduced into breeding programs. The new strains increased genetic diversity of many new varieties. Some of the strains developed during this period include Skunk #1, White Widow and Silver Haze.

By the time the third wave took hold, the goals of the second wave had been achieved. Height, light requirements, yield, and potency were all improved. Plants required only 60 to 70 days to mature, and provided much greater yields than the second wave varieties. Some of these changes were masked as the seed companies quietly improved old varieties based on new, higher standards. While keeping an eye on improving plant characteristics, breeders took more interest in flavors, tastes and aromas, which in the eyes of connoisseurs loosely correspond with the high.

This book is about the fourth wave. These strains come from breeders whose experiences have been with modern domesticated strains. They use them as building blocks, occasionally adding early classics or landraces to the mix.

Fourth-wave plants are tweaked to produce connoisseur highs. Like cooks adding spices, breeders cross the plants and re-cross them using the art and science of breeding techniques. The result can be a delight to the senses and the mind. These complex varieties contain combinations of THC and aromatics which trigger our brains to new and better highs.

You may have noticed that I mentioned THC and aromatics, but didn't mention the complex recipe of cannabinoids that mediate the high. Recent research shows that most modern marijuana varieties contain very small amounts of most cannabinoids other than THC. Other research shows that CBD, which has long been suspected of mediating the high in some way, has medicinal properties but does not affect the high at all.

If THC is the only cannabinoid present in most marijuana and the only difference in the THC is the percentage in a particular sample, what makes varieties differ in the effects? The high, the mood and the body effects differ by variety and even by growing technique. The main suspects are the aromatic essences.

As we have done in earlier volumes, *Big Book of Buds 3* surveys new varieties and articles of interest. Our theme this time is the plant and its chemical relationship to humans. It all starts with the mystery of the seed, which contains the plant's blueprint. We then take a look at something new under the sun: feminized seeds. What are they, and are they good for you? Next, we examine the issue of stability. What does it mean? Why is it important? How can you use it to your advantage? In a longer piece, we sniff out the magic of marijuana's essential oils: terpenes, terpinoids, sesqueterpenoids and other volatiles. These essences that give each variety a general aroma and each plant its individual bouquet could also affect its high. We will speculate on the bigger significance that flavor may have on marijuana's effects. Finally, we take a close look at trichomes, breaking down the differences in marijuana's glands in words and terrific photos.

You may now enter the labyrinth.

The icon section can be used as a quick key to varieties. It is expanded in this edition to include feminized seed.

The Icons

The first icon deals with plant type. The possibilities are:

This icon indicates that the company offers only feminized seeds of this variety. Feminized seeds are the result of a cross between a regular female and male-induced pollen on a second female, resulting in 100% female seeds. For more information on the way seeds are feminized, see the essay on this topic, page 148. Feminized seeds are great for the gardener that does not want to sex plants. Breeders may want a mix of male and female seeds for their purposes.

S represents plants with over 80% sativa background

I with a background of 80% or more indica

Hybrids which are:

S I more sativa

I S more indica

I Indica plants originated around the 30th parallel in the Hindu Kush region of the Himalayan foothills. This includes the countries of Afghanistan, Pakistan, Tajikistan, Northern India and Nepal. The weather there is quite variable from year to year. For this reason the populations there have a varied gene pool and even within a particular population there is a high degree of heterogeneity, which results in plants of the same variety having quite a bit of variability. This helps the population survive. No matter what the weather during a particular year, some plants will survive and reproduce.

These plants are fairly short, usually under 5 feet tall. They are bushy with compact branching and short internodes. They range in shape from a rounded bush to a pine-like shape with a wide base. The leaves are short, very wide and a darker shade of green than most equatorial sativas because they contain larger amounts of chlorophyll. Sometimes there is webbing between the leaflets. At the 30th latitude, the plants don't receive as much light as plants at or near the equator. By increasing the amount of chlorophyll, the cells use light more efficiently.

Indica buds are dense and tight. They form several shapes depending on variety. All of them are chunky or blocky. Sometimes they form continuous clusters along the stem. They have intense smells ranging from acrid, skunky, musky, to other equally pungent aromas. Indica smoke is dense, lung expanding and cough inducing. The high is heavy, body-oriented and lethargic.

S Sativa plants grow from the equator through the 50th parallel. They include both marijuana and hemp varieties. The plants that interest marijuana growers come from the equator to the 20th parallel. Countries from this area are noted for high-grade marijuana and include Colombia, Jamaica, Nigeria, Congo, Thailand, and Sumatra. Populations of plants from most of these areas are quite uniform for several reasons. Cannabis is not native to these areas. It was imported to grow hemp crops and then it adapted over many generations with human intervention. Each population originated from a small amount of fairly uniform seed from the 45-50th parallel. Then the populations evolved over hundreds of generations with the help of humans. This led to fairly uniform populations in climates that varied little year to year.

Sativas grow into 5-15 feet tall symmetrical pine-shaped plants. The spaces between the leaves on the stem, the internodes, are longer on sativas than indicas. This helps give sativas a taller stature. The lowest branches are the widest, spreading $1^1/_2$ to 3 feet; since the branches grow opposite each other, plant diameter may reach 6 feet. The leaves are long, slender and finger-like. The plants are light green since they contain less chlorophyll.

Sativa buds are lighter than indicas. Some varieties grow buds along the entire branch, developing a thin but dense cola. Others grow large formations of very light buds. The smoke is sweet, spicy or fruity. The highs are described as soaring, psychedelic, thoughtful and spacy.

Indica-sativa hybrids naturally tend towards the indica side of the family. They usually have controlled height. They don't grow very tall and after forcing flowering, their growth is limited. Their side branching is usually not prominent and they can be grown in a small space.

Sativa-indica hybrids tend towards the sativa parentage. They are taller plants, which will grow to double or triple their size if they are forced when they are small. They are usually hard to grow in a sea of green, as the plants demand more space to spread out.

With the many combinations and complex parentages of modern hybrids, it is impossible to generalize about the qualities of hybrids' smoke, highs or other characteristics. So many plants have been crossed and their progeny used for breeding that it is truly a mixed-up world out there. The *Big Book of Buds* series answers your questions regarding characteristics of particular varieties.

 The second icon details the number of days it takes the plant to ripen after forcing flowering. Some outdoor strains also offer the approximate time of harvest. Both environmental conditions and subjective factors affect maturation.

Take, for instance, one experiment in which identical plants grown indoors in a lab were fed different water-soluble commercial fertilizers. These identical plants grown with identical conditions save the fertilizers ripened up to 10 days apart. The fertilizers also affected the taste and quality of the buds.

Plant growth and maturation is also affected by temperature. Both cold and hot conditions interfere with ripening. Temperate conditions encourage fast growth and prompt ripening. The planting method is another factor in ripening time. Hydroponic plants mature earlier than their sisters in planting medium.

I would call a plant ripe when the "resin" in the glands starts to turn milky or amber. This is about a week later than some people prefer. The taste differs and the cannabinoids may change a bit, resulting in different highs. Dutch coffeeshops often sell bud that is immature. The glands are there, but have not filled completely with THC. The high is racing and buzzy. I don't find it that satisfying. Obviously, ripening time is affected by your idea of ripeness. There is more information on glands and ripeness in the essay "What Are Trichomes?"

It is easy to see that the numbers mentioned are intended to give the reader an approximation rather than hard figures. While they offer an indication of what you should expect, they shouldn't be used to figure your timetable.

Plants that are recommended for growing outdoors indicate the maturity date under natural light. When no latitude is mentioned, figure the month indicated is at the same latitude as the country of origin. For Holland, the latitude is 52 degrees. Canadian seeds are produced at the 50 degree latitude, the U.S. at the 38 degree latitude, and Spanish seeds are produced at the 40-41 degrees latitude. More can be found about outdoor harvest times and latitude in the appendices.

The third icon indicates recommendations for planting. The choices are:

 indoor

 outdoor

 indoor/outdoor

Outdoor strains may do well in a greenhouse setup, but will be difficult to grow indoors. They may require too much light for inside growing, and usually have their own ideas about growth and height, making them hard to tame. The problem with most plants not recommended for outdoors in temperate climates is that the plants don't ripen by the end of the season. Some plants rated as indoor plants can be grown outdoors if they are forced to flower early using shade cloth. As an example, a plant which ripens in mid-November, 45 days after a gardener's September 30th harvest schedule, could be coaxed to flower early by covering it with opaque plastic each evening after sunset. Remove the cover 12 hours after sunset, beginning in late spring or early summer. Most varieties ripen in 60-70 days.

The fourth icon is a report of expected yield. These figures are somewhat ambiguous since the results are not reported consistently. Cannabis, as all green plants, uses light to fuel photosynthesis. The sugars produced become tissue. As a shortcut, you could say Light = Growth. Yields vary first and foremost due to light conditions, so space or plant definitions are incomplete by themselves. The yields that appear here assume that indoor gardens are receiving at least 600 watts per meter (wpm) where no light wattage is indicated.

The fifth icon is listed only on plants suitable for sea of green gardens. Plants in these gardens are spaced together very closely so that each plant needs to grow little if any to fill the canopy. Plants are forced to flower soon after they are placed in the flowering space. Eliminating the vegetative growth stage decreases turnaround. SOG gardens hold 3 to 6 plants per square foot.

The sixth icon is the parentage of the variety. While this can get quite complex, you get an idea of what the possibilities are for any variety by knowing its parents.

Some of the hybrids in the book are F2 unstabilized. When pure strains (let's call them strains A & B) are crossed and a hybrid is produced, the first generation, the F1 hybrid plants, are all uniform because they all contain the same genes. One set from the female and one set from the male. When two F1's are crossed, the seeds receive a random assortment of genes. For each of the more than 100,000 sets of genes, a plant may get two genes from A one each from A and B or two from B. No two plants are alike.

To stabilize them so that they have similar characteristics, the plants are inbred for five or six generations creating an F6, using careful selections. However, breeders often work with unstabilized hybrids, which has an advantage when breeding for cloning.

Stability can be judged in part by the number of parents a variety has. Pure strains are the most uniform, since they are not recombining different genetic dispositions. Hybrids have the advantage of gaining vigor from fresh combinations. They also vary more. Strains with three or four parents are likely to exhibit more than one phenotype when grown out. When the three parents are hybrids themselves, the combination can result in quite a bit of diversity.

Diversity is not bad. Consider a gardener starting out. Clones are taken once the plants grow some side stems. When the plants have been harvested and tasted the gardener decides to select two plants for the next garden. Clones of those plants are grown vegetatively and used for mothers. If the seed line were uniform as it is with pure strains or stabilized varieties, there would not be much difference between the plants. Seeds from an unstabilized variety gives the gardener more choices.

The seventh icon is the one that is most important to me. What is the high like? Describing a state of mind is not an easy task. Separating one's mind state from the state of mind created by the brain in interplay with the cannabinoids is subtle. We have used many terms to describe these states:

alert • body relaxation • body stone • cerebral • cheerful • clear head • couch lock • creative • creeper • creepy and sleepy • energetic • euphoric • even body/head high • giggly • ha-ha • happy • lethargic • mellowing • munchie • narcotic • physically relaxing • psychedelic • sleepy • social • stoney • trippy • uplifting • visual and wandering mind
These are icons of mental states. The text contains more complete descriptions.

The eighth icon, the final one, is a short, 1-3 word description of the smell and taste. The odors we included are:

acrid • ammonia • berry • blueberry • bubblegum • citrus • dry spicy • earthy • floral • fruity • hashy • chocolate • mango • melon • minimal • musky • old sock • peppery • pineapple • piney • pungent • skunk • smooth • spicy • spicy sandalwood • sweet • tart fruit candy • tobacco • tropical sweet • woodsy • and woodsy fresh.

Once again fuller descriptions are found in the text. You will find the description of odors and ter-

penes on page 96 most informative.

The icons are fast reference points. They give you an idea of where the story is going. The text accompanying the variety fleshes out this information with more nuanced descriptions and tips about the plants preferences. Every story offers something a little different. Still we have to admit that we love the photos the most. They show what words can only attempt to express. I'm sure they will provide you with hours of sightseeing pleasure.

Quick Key to Icons

Strain Type

Sativa

Indica

Sativa/Indica

Indica/Sativa

Sativa/Ruderalis

Indica/Ruderalis

Feminized

Growing Info

Flowering time
Tiempo de floración
Blütezeit
Durée de floraison
Stagione della fioritura
Bloetijd

Parents
Genética
Mutterpflanze
Descendance
Genitori
Stamboom

Yield
Rendimiento
Ertag
Rendement
Raccolta
Opbrengst

Sea of Green

Indoor
Interior
Drinnen
d'Intérieur
Dentro
Binnen

Outdoor
Exterior
Draussen
d'Extérieur
Fuori
Buiten

Indoor/Outdoor
Interior/Exterior
Drinnen/Draussen
d'Intérieur/d'Extérieur
Dentro/Fuori
Binnen/Buiten

Sensory Experience

Buzz
Efecto
die Art des Turns
Effets
Effetti
High Effekt

Taste/Smell
Sabor/Aroma
Geschmack/Geruch
Saveur/Arôme
Sapore/Odore
Smaak/Geua

Breeder Location

Australia

Canada

Netherlands

Spain

United Kingdom

U.S.A.

A-Train • Afropips First Grade Malawi Go
Arjans Haze #1 • Arjans Haze #2 • A
BC Blueberry • BC God Bud • BC Swee
Blue Buddha • Blue Cheese • Brainston
Chrystal • Cinderella 99 x Panama Red •
First Lady • Fruit of the Gods • Fruity Tha
Grape Ape • Grape Krush • Hashberry
Jack the Ripper • Jacky White • Jilly
Kiwiskunk • Kushage • LA Confidential •
Green • Motavation • Mothers Finest •
Purple Kush • Sadhu • Somaui • Somini
Queen • Spoetnik #1 • Sputnik • (Arjan
Church • The Doctor • The Purps • T
(Arjans) Ultra Haze #1 • (Arjans) Ultra
Wappa • White Berry • White Smurf • Wh

Varieties

AK-48 • American Dream • Arctic Sun
ans Haze #3 • Aurora Borealis • B-52
Tooth • Big Bang • Big Buddha Cheese
Haze • Burmese Kush • Casey Jones
D-Line • Ed Rosenthal Super Bud • F-13
• G-13 Diesel • Gonzo #1 • Grandaddy
Hash Heaven • Haze Mist • Ice Cream
ean • Kaya • KC-36 • KC-45 • Kish
owryder #2 • Mako Haze • Mazar • Man
Mount Cook • Nuken • Opium • Posh
Sour Cream • (IBL) Sour Diesel • Speed
Strawberry Haze • Sweet 105 • The
e Third Dimension • TNR • True Blue
Haze #2 • Venus • Very Berry Haze
e Rhino • White Satin • Wonder Woman

A-Train

TH Seeds

All aboard! The A-Train is about to take you on a journey from the rolling hills of northern California through the Mazar-i-Sharif mountains of Afghanistan, finally arriving in the Low Countries of Europe. This California-Afghani F1 hybrid was bred in Holland for indoor grows. A-Train's father comes from Afghanistan's hash heartland, while her California mom is Trainwreck, a clone-only variety from the West Coast medical marijuana community renowned for an excellent high and refreshing flavor.

A-Train performs best as a multi-branch plant. She is a space hog, with extensive lower branching and a tendency to sprawl and lean. Supports or netting are recommended for those who want their girls to be orderly. If allowed to grow without control, her branches will probably still need rearranging in order to maximize light for the buds. No matter how she is trained, it is advisable to trim off the lower branches, reserving energy for bud formations on her upper levels.

Gardeners who prioritize yield should consider hydroponics for this strain, while those in search of primo flavors do better with soil. Either way, A-Train loves organic foods. When growing hydroponically, TH Seeds prefers Botanicare Pure Blend Pro and Liquid Karma to pump up the enzymes. During peak flowering times, they use Bud Swell. A-Train will become finicky and troublesome if exposed to too much humidity. Otherwise, she is a clean, dry, and relatively non-smelly plant.

This strain finishes in $7^1/_2$ to $8^1/_2$ weeks. She more than quadruples in height during that time, starting when she is forced – beginning the flowering cycle at one foot (30 cm) will result in plants that are $4^1/_2$ to 5 feet (1.3 to 1.5m) at finish. As she grows, this lanky brancher takes on a gauzy green coloration, and tends to form many plantlet buds. If she is pruned to a single-cola plant, A-Train will produce 25-35 grams (approx. 1 oz.) per plant. When grown in 1-gallon containers in soil, she yields 35-55 grams per plant, and

50S/50I

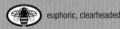
euphoric, clearheaded

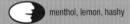
menthol, lemon, hashy

53-60 days

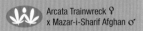
Arcata Trainwreck ♀
x Mazar-i-Sharif Afghan ♂

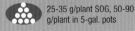
25-35 g/plant SOG, 50-90
g/plant in 5-gal. pots

5-gallon potted plants can deliver between 50 and 90 grams (2-3 oz.) apiece.

The harvested buds are round and compact, resembling clusters of green walnuts coated with a silver shellac of resin. On the menthol-lemon inhale, A-Train brings you a satisfying, well balanced mind and body lift, a clear and and productive high. On the exhale of lip-numbing sweetness with bits of Afghan hashi-ness, A-Train brings you home; you can drop your baggage from the day. This strain's creeper high will gradually slow you down a notch or two, but it won't stun you into a stupor. It's a combination of two strains used widely by the medical pot community for alleviating mind and body discomfort.

Afropips First Grade Malawi Gold

Afropips Seeds

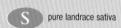 pure landrace sativa

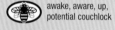 awake, aware, up, potential couchlock

 spicy, tropical

 80-120 days

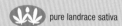 pure landrace sativa

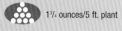 1³/₄ ounces/5 ft. plant

Malawi Gold is a foundational landrace strain that has been cultivated for centuries in one of the world's cannabis sweet spots, the east African country of Malawi (formerly Nyasaland). Traditionally grown outdoors using open pollination methods, this strain's gene pool developed variable grades and potencies. Afropips' Malawi Gold comes from the high quality Mother Trees growers and is great for breeding vigor and potency into new hybrid varieties.

Malawi Gold seeds have a caruncle or point of attachment at their base that is uncommonly deep, and often surrounded by a sharp edged lip. Seeds are large, shortened, flattened and ovoid in shape. They germinate best in a warm soil medium with seedlings visible above the surface after 2-3 days.

Although it prefers soil, Afropips First-Grade Malawi Gold still thrives using other growing methods. When grown outdoors in its home environment, it can reach 13 feet (4 m) supported by stems like tree trunks and yields in the kilograms. It is a vigorous plant that exhibits good pest and mold resistance, stands up well to adverse temperature changes and bounces back fast from damage, giving it the reputation as the "lazy man's" plant in Malawi. When grown indoors, or outdoors in northern latitudes, its longer sativa growing season and its tendencies to height and branchiness requires attention.

Malawi Gold will shoot up and stretch throughout its growing cycles. It takes 12-18 weeks to mature. If seeds are started in soil and shuttled immediately into flowering cycle without a vegetative period, they will reach a height of about 5 feet (1.5 m) and yield about 1³/₄ ounces (50 g) of dried bud per plant. Afropips has selectively bred a bushier, more compact Malawi Gold phenotype for indoor growers. This indoor strain reaches only 3 feet (1 m) at maturity, making it appropriate for growers with height restrictions.

This lovely sativa is fresh grass green with coarsely serrated, thin leaflets that hang in a narrow, drooping, hand-like array. The leaves lack serrations on the tips, which are very long and comprise 20% of each leaflet. The stems and fan leaf stalks often have a burgundy red striping. The overall structure and shape is a willowy Christmas tree.

Mature Malawi Gold sensimilla floral clusters are airy as a result of the sativa's long internodes. While growing, the stems produce the unique Malawi musky scent with hints of cinnamon. Developing and ripe buds are earthy, and cured buds have a characteristic Malawi spiciness that would be best described as exotic and luxuriant. The buzz is the epitome of sativa—an alert mental clarity coupled with a warm pleasant feeling that radiates throughout the body. Smooth and mellow, this variety can also reach into the spacey and psychedelic regions. Effects are exaggerated by longer curing times, and the onset and duration of the buzz are elongated. Sometimes buds that have cured longer can take on a slight couch-lock effect. Overall this is a motivational strain appropriate for most activities. Afropips particularly recommends sensory indulgences with your sweetheart or dancing to Reggae music.

Afroman & the Malawi Gold

Raised in Africa, the Afroman started smoking Durban Poison in his hometown in the late 1970s. After systematically working his way through Transkei, Swazi, Lesotho, Mozambique, Zambia & Zimbabwean weed, he ended up settling for his personal favorite— Malawi. Malawi Gold has been the Afroman's first choice and everyday weed since 1985.

Southern Africa is renowned for its stock of pure sativa strains. Malawi plants are tall and elegant with slender leaves and pale green buds. They often develop pink and purple coloring when ripe, and have a distinct full-palate flavor that mixes the floral sweet of sativa with a little spice. Malawi Gold got its name because the buds are traditionally cured by binding them in maize leaves. When finished they are compressed and turn a golden hue reminiscent of fall leaves. The Malawi variety has gained a reputation among travelers for the deliciously sativa, "up" high and the distinctive golden tones.

Afroman relocated to England in the year 2000. Love of ganja got the Afroman growing and his personal taste and medical preferences gave him the breeding bug. He likes to maintain a perpetual garden with seven harvests a year. Special plants that are harvested at the beginning of the year are regenerated and reharvested at the end of the year. He specializes in African landraces and his mission is preserving and creating New African hybrids. Afroman says that his first wife is Mary Jane, and his harem and offspring stretch to the four corners of the planet.

AK-48

Nirvana Seed Bank

Since the mid 1990's "AK" strains have been increasingly popular. The Nirvana AK-48 is a strong early finishing version. Its ICE mother has ancestors of Afghani, Skunk, Northern Lights and Shiva stock. An intense selection process drawing from thousands of plants was used to find this special mother. ICE flowers are richly covered in trichomes and have a dense consistency. She has a high flower-to-leaf ratio, with buds forming along her main branches. The father is Jock Horror, a three-way hybrid that combines genetics from Northern Lights, Skunk and Haze. The Jock Horror is a heavy resin producer and an early finisher with a unique fresh flavor and a potent upbeat buzz.

From these parents, the AK-48 has retained a fast finish, producing hard buds that have an exceptional and penetrating aroma. Although she is a mix of indica and sativa with a slight indica dominance genetically, AK-48 retains key sativa qualities in her high. AK-48 finishes in as early as 7 weeks if conditions are perfect, but otherwise may take as long as 9 weeks to finish.

This variety is optimally grown indoors using a soil medium and organic fertilizers to get the best flavor, although her flavor is considered secondary to her punchy buzz and fast grow time. She is great for sea-of-green style gardens. Nirvana recommends planting 16 plants per square meter, then pruning each plant to only 6 branches and the top in order to optimize the size and bud consistency throughout the crop. AK-48 is a medium-sized plant that will double in height if flowering is induced at 20 inches (50 cm). The leaves on this plant are small, somewhat thin, and delicate. Outdoors, it is particularly suitable for climates such as Spain, where it finishes in October. Overall, this plant is hardy yet manageable, bouncing back well from minor stresses. For this reason, it is a good choice for a beginner who likes a buzz with a slow onset and a strong kick once it takes effect.

 65I/35S

 cerebral

 earthy sativa

 49-63 days

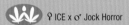 ♀ ICE x ♂ Jock Horror

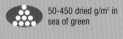 50-450 dried g/m² in sea of green

 SOG

American Dream

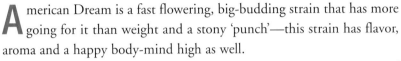

American Dream is a fast flowering, big-budding strain that has more going for it than weight and a stony 'punch'—this strain has flavor, aroma and a happy body-mind high as well.

American Dream performs reliably for first-time growers in a range of conditions, overcoming any number of small imperfections and still producing a harvest of potent, fragrant flowers. In the hands of a more experienced grower, American Dream can really shine, and should be a breath of fresh air to anyone who thinks that all new hybrids are the same. An ideal plant for indoors, American Dream is very responsive to training and an excellent choice for the sea of green (SOG) method because she gains more height than a pure indica, but will not grow out of control when flowered at normal SOG sizes. She can be trained to stay small or allowed to grow into a large plant with multiple stems. In warm climates or greenhouses, this plant flourishes, with mature outdoor heights reaching 4 to 8 feet (125-250 cm).

The skunk heritage is evident in this plant's structure and growth patterns. American Dream has strong stems, short internode gaps and a fast, powerful indica-type growth at all stages. Mid-stem branches can grow nearly as tall as her central cola and may need support in late flowering as the buds start to gain bulk. Sativa influences can be seen in the calyx/bud formation and are present in the THC content. Individual tops are dense and fat, creating an interesting pyramid shape as they form—their round, oversized calyxes 'bubble' up to a blunt peak, and the way they stack atop each other gives the appearance of three or four triangular, almost-flat surfaces leading to the apex. When these polygonal chunks grow, they coalesce into long, thick cylinders of dewy bud. Small growths pop out from the main cola at every angle like kernels of corn popping on the cob. The medium green of these buds is glazed with a thick, quicksilver sheen of resin, making them terrific for hash hopefuls or cannabis cooks. Processing buds and small leaves will yield a

 70I/30S

 talkative, happy

 citrus skunk

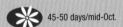 45-50 days/mid-Oct.

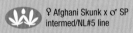 ♀ Afghani Skunk x ♂ SP intermed/NL#5 line

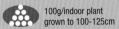 100g/indoor plant grown to 100-125cm

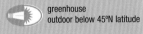 greenhouse outdoor below 45°N latitude

 SOG

significant amount of superb hashish, but even growers who don't take this step can salvage plenty of finger hash during the manicure.

American Dream's citrusy high comes on like the proverbial ton of bricks. Normal consumption should not be incapacitating for the average smoker, but it might be a better strain in familiar and stress-free surroundings. The effect is less up or down, than sideways. Neither hyper nor sleepy, American Dream tends to simply shift things into a new perspective that increases a feeling of being "in the moment," making it an enhancement for getting caught up in a film, book, favorite CD or video game.

American Dream

We named this variety "American Dream" because a room or garden full of these ladies is a beautiful expression of life, liberty and the pursuit of happiness, even if the plants themselves are forbidden under the current interpretation of that creed.

The American Dream is built on beliefs like self-improvement and self-reliance; a person's inherent right to do what they wish, provided it harms no one else; the idea that the most modest beginnings can blossom into bountiful rewards through the application of honest work.

The American Dream seed-strain is named because it, along with all lovingly-grown cannabis around the world, represents and embodies those values so well.

Arctic Sun

Flying Dutchmen

 60S/40I

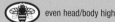 even head/body high

 fuel, floral

 56-70 days/end Oct.

 ♀ White Widow (P1) x ♂ Skunk #1 (P1)

 1 g/watt of light used

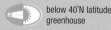 below 40°N latitude greenhouse

Arctic Sun is a combination of two powerhouses of the Dutch seed-breeding establishment—Skunk #1 and White Widow—which have been used extensively in Holland to create high yielding, potent strains. The White Widow mother has been in Flying Dutchmen's library for over a decade. Originally a South Indian/Brazilian hybrid, the mother plant boasts a 12-week maturation time, extreme potency and a high yield. Crossing this strain with a strong skunk father produces a 60/40 sativa/indica plant that can be grown indoors in a greenhouse or outdoors at a latitude below 40 degrees North.

Indoors this plant gives the best results when grown without pruning at a density of 12-16 plants per square meter. Trimming off all the lower shoots at the base of the plants allows for more airflow and focuses the growth at the top. Arctic Sun usually finishes with a central calyx and 6-8 side branches, at a height of around 2-2³/₄ feet (60-80 cm) with the lowest 1 foot (30 cm) bare. The usual yields are 1¹/₂ -1³/₄ ounces (40-50 g) per plant at 600 watts of light per square meter.

After testing Arctic Sun in most mediums, Flying Dutchmen recommends growing in pre-dressed soil high in organic matter, although high quality yields are also common in coco fiber and rockwool. Arctic Sun has a fairly dense growth pattern during vegetative growth, with short internode spaces and medium-dark green, mid-sized leaflets and longish petioles, maturing into short to medium height plants with compact buds that have large bracts and few pistils.

Outdoors the unpruned Arctic Sun matures into a stocky 6-foot (2.5 m) Christmas tree with occasional purple coloration. Yields outdoors can be spectacular during a good season; greenhouse plants have weighed in at 22-24 ounces (650-700 g) per plant in Holland. Artic Sun thrives on fairly high nutrient levels. Special care should be taken to flush plants in the last 10-14 days for optimum taste. Although some plants in the population finish at 8 weeks, the nicest plants for selection tend to be fully mature at 9 weeks. In Holland, Arctic Sun matures at the end of October.

At harvest, Arctic Sun has an aroma that is balanced between her parents: a pungent fuel-like tang with surprising floral undertones. The buds are dense, greasy and very heavy. When cured, the buds mellow a little, leaving a perfect balance of potency and everyday enjoyability.

Tastewise, the curry house pungency is tempered by the sweetness of the Skunk #1. The Artic Sun is loved by smokers with high tolerance levels. The high is both cerebral and physical and can be enjoyed over time without developing a threshold. The cannabinoid profile of the Artic Sun lends itself well to medical applications for chronic pain, spasms associated with MS and sleeplessness.

Arjan's Haze #1

Green House Seed Company

Photos: Jan Otsen

Green House Seed Company caters to the haze fan with several strains in this family. Arjan's Haze #1 is a strong sativa with medium-size internodes, a combination of G-13 and Neville's Haze. Hazes tend to be a bit leggy, because they branch rapidly, forming a lanky pine tree shape. Arjan's Haze #1 is in the middle of the haze spectrum and can be kept short by pruning and splitting. The stems are very flexible during vegetative growth, allowing for easy bending and training. Ideally this plant is grown with two plants per square yard (meter^2).

The best yields for this variety come from hydro systems, but growing in soil will give a smoother taste and a more natural high. It can be grown with sufficient indoor space, or outside in Mediterranean, temperate and subtropical regions. Arjan's Haze #1 has a very fast metabolism and absorbs more feedings than the average sativa. Green House recommends starting with a low pH (5.5 hydro/ 5.7 soil) and slowly increasing to 6.3 at the end of flowering. Maximum EC levels should be 2.1 in hydro and 1.9 in soil. Plants should be flushed in the final stages of flowering.

As haze cultivators know, these special sativas require longer grow times. Arjan's Haze #1 ripens in an average 11 weeks, or late October/early November in the northern hemisphere. When planted in 5-gallon (20-liter) containers, this plant will reach a leggy 8-9 feet (250-270 cm) at harvest. In smaller, 2-gallon (7.5-liter) containers, height can be limited to 4-5 feet (120-150 cm) at maturity. When root development is not limited and ideal conditions are met, this plant can easily reach over 10 feet (3 m).

This dark oily green plant has large leaves and huge buds that are quite compact and dense for a sativa, with an irregular shape due to calyx development, and short thick hairs. Its intense sativa aromas – reminding one of moss, forest, and musk – are a natural deterrant to pests. The smoke has a background of incense and hard wood, with hints of mint and pepper in flavor. Its strong high creeps up slowly and steadily, reaching a very long peak. It is an uplifting and clearheaded sensation that is ideal for social activities.

 S I 80S/20I

 strong, up, social

 moss, forest

 77 days

 ♀ Neville's Haze x ♂G13 sativa

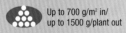 Up to 700 g/m² in/ up to 1500 g/plant out

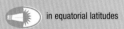 in equatorial latitudes

Arjan's Haze #2 ♀♀

Green House Seed Company

Photos: Jan Otsen

 S I 90S/10I

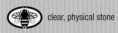 clear, physical stone

 woody musk

 77 days

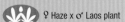 ♀ Haze x ♂ Laos plant

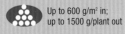 Up to 600 g/m² in; up to 1500 g/plant out

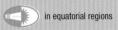 in equatorial regions

Arjan's Haze #2 is a rich dark green near-pure sativa with a haze mama, and a papa hailing from the Southeast Asian country of Laos. With partial heredity in the subtropics, this plant performs best outdoors in the equatorial regions, the Mediterranean, and some mild but temperate regions to the north. Arjan's Haze #2 has large internodes and lanky branches that tend to shoot out, forming a typical pine-tree shape. It can be acclimated to an indoor grow if the garden space has tall ceilings or if the gardener can apply bending techniques (this is easiest during vegetative growth, when her branches are very flexible). Her height can also be controlled by limiting root development. In small (2-gal.) containers, the plant reaches a mature height of 4-5 feet (120-150 cm); in 5-gallon containers she will grow to 9-10 feet (270-300 cm). Once flowering, her combo of weighty buds and bendy branches will benefit from staking and support.

Green House suggests two plants every three square feet as an ideal grow setup. Arjan's Haze #2 has a very sativa metabolism, so it absorbs feedings well but does not need high EC levels. The maximum EC should be 1.8 in hydro and 1.6 in soil. Adequate flushing to remove traces of salts should be provided every 10-14 days.

This variety ripens in 11 weeks. Arjan's Haze #2 tends to keep flowering on the main cola after the lower branches have reached ripeness. Outdoors, it will ripen between the end of October and the beginning of November, reaching heights over 10 feet (3 m). Her colas tend to be very long and dense for a sativa, and can have quite irregular shapes due to their wild calyx development. The hairs are thick and long, and the leaves are huge, with 11 leaflets on average at peak growth.

While this strain's high starts off clear, it is typically followed by a very strong stoned effect that can lead you to feeling rubbery in the knees. Some smokers define it as a "slap in the face" high. It is great for purely recreational activities that are not too physically taxing or highly focused in nature. Anecdotes suggest that this strain is a good medicinal selection for MS patients. Arjan's Haze #2 has a very woody flavor that reminds one of wine barrels, musk and incense, with a background scent of lavender.

The Mystery of the Seed

Ed Rosenthal

Marijuana is probably the single most anthropomorphized plant. There are many reasons to imagine marijuana's comparisons with human qualities. First, marijuana is an annual that completes its life cycle, from seed to plant to seed again, in a few months. You could say that every two days or so in the life of a marijuana plant is equal to a year of human life. Second, cannabis is dioecious, meaning that plants are separated into males and females. Third, the sexes are dimorphic: their life cycles are somewhat different and their appearances diverge as they age. Marijuana is the only annual that has two sexes.

Seeds being sorted from plant matter in Morocco's Rif Mountains.

Cultivation techniques also push us to think of marijuana somewhat differently from any other domesticated plant. Almost all other harvests, such as fruits and grains, are the bounty of fertilized flowers. However, marijuana harvests are best when the plant is kept from reproducing. To prevent this pollination, we treat the plant more like a member of the family than a farm crop. We limit her contact with the opposite sex and prevent sexual relations. The goal: virgin buds unspoiled by pollen.

We share an emotional tie with marijuana because of its ability to affect us subjectively. As a result, we sometimes think of the plants themselves as individuals, even naming them. Such names often denote our individual experiences or the sexuality of the plant.

As with humans, the reproductively ready female form of cannabis is the most desired, or at least most depicted and venerated in imagery. In most other mammals, as well as fish, birds, and reptiles, the male is usually on exhibition.

Our familiarity and symbiotic relationship with marijuana have made the plant seem like a friend, albeit one that can get you in a lot of trouble. Step back for just a minute and set aside your warm emotions. Take a fresh look at marijuana, and you will discover an organism from the plant kingdom that parallels our life form.

The Plant and the Seed

Do chickens produce eggs to make more chickens? Or do eggs produce chickens to make more eggs? It may seem like a frivolous question, until it is examined more deeply. The entire life of a plant, from seed to expiration, is spent mostly as an embryo enclosed in a pod. As soon as the seed germinates the plant begins its quest to grow and produce more seed before it dies.

As in human reproduction, the cannabis seed or embryo is the result of a complex set of parallel processes by the male and female reproductive organs, the flowers. Male flower buds look something like pawnbroker's balls. They hang down from the stem. As the five-petal white or cream colored flowers open they move to face upward, making it easy for the breeze to carry away the pollen. Each pollen grain contains two sperm cells. They are haploid, meaning each holds half a set of chromosomes.

Once it catches the wind, the pollen floats until it is caught on an object. A small percentage alight on a

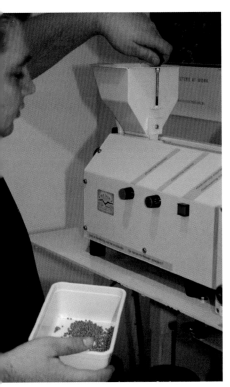

Seeds being loaded into a seed packaging machine.

female flower's stigma. The female flower has no petals. It consists of two stigmas topping styles that attach to the ovary. A single ovule (think egg) also contains a haploid number of chromosomes.

When a pollen grain lands on a virgin stigma it is

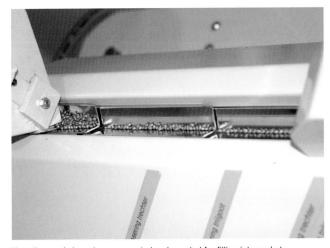

Here the seeds have been seperated and counted for filling into packets.

Seed packets ready for shipment.

Longitudinal Section of a Seed

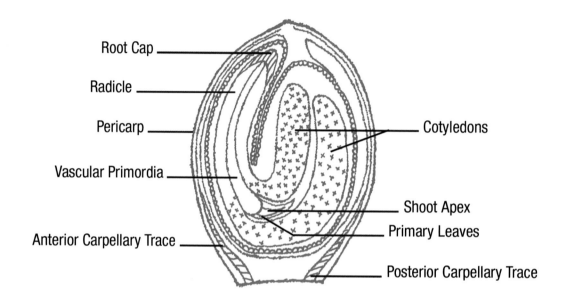

Root Cap

Radicle

Pericarp

Vascular Primordia

Anterior Carpellary Trace

Cotyledons

Shoot Apex

Primary Leaves

Posterior Carpellary Trace

hydrated by a sugary liquid provided by its host. Once germinated, it grows a pollen tube that follows a path through the style to the ovary, where the single ovule is attached to the placenta at the base of the ovary's inner wall. The two sperm travel down the tube. One of them combines with the ovule to form the embryo. The other sperm combines with several eggs that have been modified in development, become infertile and gathered high energy food and tissue that lines the ovary called "endosperm." The embryo grows as it receives nourishment from the plant through the placenta and it incorporates some of the endosperm. The rest is used for nourishment during germination. The pericarp, the seed coat, which has developed from the ovary's outer wall, begins to harden as the seed matures and breaks away from the placenta, which dries up. The seed is now mature.

Encased inside its hard shell, the embryo is in a state of near suspended animation. It can remain viable frozen for years and can survive heat spells as well. It is activated when the outer case is hydrated in warm temperatures, above 50°F (10°C). Within minutes of being moistened, the seed prepares for germination, which becomes visible as the tap root breaks the hard shell and emerges a few days later.

Seeds ready for germination.

We may think that our brains make the important decisions of our lives, but for the most part they have been made for us, hardwired in genetic codes. For all our efforts, our consciousness cannot alter our path through life — fetus, infant, toddler, child, adolescent, adult, geriatric, dead. Our growth and reproductive patterns are conveyer belts that never stop. Luckily, our brains don't have much to say about how to grow teeth, where to place our eyes or how our digestive system works, because to the extent that it is able to interfere, it usually messes up. And so it is with plants — they are pre-programmed to respond to environmental conditions in ways that echo what their progenitors experienced for the past millions of years. When you think about it, we are no better adapted to the environment than cannabis. We are all survivors. The rest are called extinct.

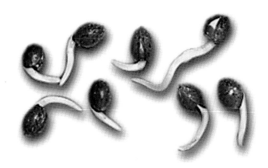

Germination begins when the root emerges from the seed.

You can see the pericap of the seed still on top of the embryonic leaf, the cotyledon. The first true leaves are visible above the cotyledon.

Photos: John Alexander

19

Arjan's Haze #3 ♀♀

Green House Seed Company

Photos: Jan Otsen

A rjan's Haze #3 brings together a father from Laos with a combination of Neville's Haze and Super Silver Haze. Green House Seed Company recommends this little powerhouse sativa for indoor growers who want the bliss of a haze variety, but don't have the most spacious of growing areas.

Arjan's Haze #3 is very flexible during vegetative growth, which facilitates easy bending. When allowed to grow naturally, it forms the typical pine-tree sativa shape. This plant flourishes outdoors, but is short enough to be at home in an indoor garden, especially if bending techniques are used for the stretchy branching. The branches may need support as the flowers get heavy enough to perform their own, less desirable "bending technique." Indoor plants do best when grown with two plants every three square feet.

This plant's height can be further controlled by limiting root development using smaller containers. Plants in 2-gallon containers stay in the 3 or 4-foot (90-120 cm) range; plants in 5-gallon (20 L) containers come closer to 5-6 feet (150-180 cm) at harvest, and if the roots are allowed to grow without space limitations, this plant can climb to 10 feet (3 m) in height at finish.

This plant reaches optimum ripeness at the end of October or beginning of November. Indoors it takes 11 weeks from forcing. Arjan's Haze #3 buds can be quite irregular in shape and the hairs are thick and short. Toward maturation, the buds tend to get a very pointy conic shape.

Like many other near-pure sativas, Arjan's Haze #3 keeps flowering on the main cola while the lower branches are already ripe. This plant has a "very sativa" metabolism; it absorbs feedings well but does not need high EC levels. Green House recommends starting with a low pH (5.5 hydro/5.7 soil) and slowly increasing to 6.2 at the end of flowering.

 80S/20I

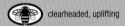 clearheaded, uplifting

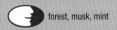 forest, musk, mint

 77 days

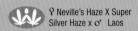 ♀ Neville's Haze X Super Silver Haze x ♂ Laos

 600 g/m²

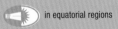 in equatorial regions

Arjan's Haze #3 has a very woody sativa flavor, a taste of musk and campfires. Underneath is a scent of mint and lemon grass. This haze delivers a potent high with the qualities that most haze fans seek: a soaring clear-headed sensation that is never too heavy on the body. This high creeps up slowly, but once its effects are felt, they stick around for a long while. It is a terrific strain for creative moods and for the euphoria it can contribute to recreational activities. Anectdotally, it has been promising for chronic pain.

Aurora Borealis

Flying Dutchmen

 50S/50I

 gentle body high

 sweet, skunky

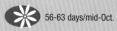 56-63 days/mid-Oct.

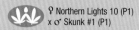 ♀ Northern Lights 10 (P1) x ♂ Skunk #1 (P1)

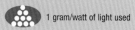 1 gram/watt of light used

 greenhouse

 SOG

Aurora Borealis is the Latin name for the natural phenomena at the North Pole otherwise known as "Northern Lights," which in turn is the name of one of this plant's celebrity parents. Northern Lights is an indica strain that, during the 1980s, made its way from the Pacific Northwest to the Netherlands, where it has become a building block for many strains around the world. The Northern Lights #10 mother was selected for commercial production back in 1997. While Northern Lights was specifically bred for the then-fledgling indoor grow scene, the other parent in this famous pair, Skunk #1, was initially bred for outdoors and greenhouse cultivation. The resulting plants are of a medium height, with dark green foliage and short internodes and a 50/50 sativa/indica phenotype expression. Aurora Borealis may have a less recognizable name than her parents, but her genetics shine through to reveal her family ties.

This strain can be grown in all suitable mediums and will thrive in most temperate regions. Outdoors, in Holland, the Aurora B. matures in mid-October. She comes up stocky with dark green foliage. Plants started in May in Holland, and left unpruned, usually finish at a height of around 5-6 feet (1.5-2 m). They yield around 300 grams per plant, weather permitting. Greenhouse yields are higher, surpassing 500 grams per plant.

Indoors, the Aurora B. performs best under a sea of green regime at a density of 16-25 plants per square meter. She thrives on generous nutrient levels and performs best in a good, rich, well aerated soil high in organic matter. Allow for a vegetative time of around 10 days or until the canopy cover is about 70% when viewed from above. Do not prune that canopy unless a longer vegetation time is required. All feeding should cease during the last 10 days of flowering so as not to impair the taste of the final product. The height of Aurora Borealis under this regime is usually around 1-2 feet (40-60 cms) and its yield ranges from 25 to 40 grams per plant, at 600 watts of light per square meter.

Once the plants mature they exhibit fairly long, broad colas with a medium density and very high resin content. The smell and taste is satisfyingly sweet, with a warm skunky undertone. The plants' odor is very pungent until fully dried and cured. Aurora B.'s high leans toward the physical, starting strong, with a long lasting and well balanced plateau and a gentle finish. Medicinally, this strain works well to alleviate symptoms for which indicas are generally prescribed, such as chronic pain, spasms, sleeplessness and nausea.

B-52

Nirvana Seed Bank

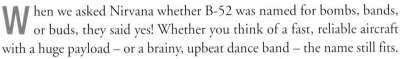

When we asked Nirvana whether B-52 was named for bombs, bands, or buds, they said yes! Whether you think of a fast, reliable aircraft with a huge payload – or a brainy, upbeat dance band – the name still fits.

B-52 is a truly superior skunk hybrid that produces consistently well and rewards the grower with a very sweet taste and a cerebral high enjoyed by connoisseurs of the skunk family strains. The maternal side of its family tree hails from Big Bud, among the oldest of the commercial strains. True to its name, Big Bud is a classic producer with little foliage to prune, plus a sweet spicy flavor and an indica-dominant body stone. Nirvana's Big Bud has been bred and selected with a priority on maximizing yields, so much so that Big Buds usually need to be staked and tied because of the heavy bud load on their branches. B-52's daddy is a Skunk Special, developed with skunk enthusiasts in mind through an intense refinement of Skunk #1. The aromatic Skunk Special fills the room with sativa pungency. With an equal presence of indica and sativa, B-52 delivers the productivity of Big Bud with the dense aromas and flavorful, mellow high of the skunks.

This plant is best for a gardener with a few crops under his or her belt. It is especially recommended for the hydro enthusiast, since B-52 gives its best yields in a hydro sea of green. Growing 16 plants per square meter and pruning the plants down to the top and four side branches achieves massive bottle-size buds. B-52 is durable and can take an EC of up to 2.6 without showing signs of overfeeding. Grown in these optimal conditions, B-52 roughly doubles in height during the flowering period and can consistently tip the scale with yields around 500 grams per square meter. While considered an indoor plant, this strain can be grown outdoors in Spain or similar climates, yielding a mature crop in the beginning of October.

Skunk lovers, especially those who like hydro, will be rewarded with good yields and sweet skunky buds. This is a good high for daydreaming, or for dancing to cheerful pop music. Rock lobster!

 IS

 all-around buzz, cerebral

 sweet

 56-70 days

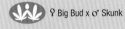 ♀ Big Bud x ♂ Skunk

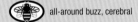 600 g/m²

 SOG

BC Blueberry

BC Bud Depot

Photos: JamJakin & BC Bud Depot

BC Bud Depot created BC Blueberry to make a renowned British Columbia clone—the only blueberry plant available in seed form. They crossed the clone plant with an unknown blueberry seed father, resulting in a mostly indica plant that is deliciously fruity sweet with just a hint of fuel.

The BC Blueberry is a moderate brancher, forming the typical triangular shape. She can also be pruned at the transition to flowering, making a nice sea of green plant. She is particular about her conditions, which makes her more appropriate for gardeners with a little experience or a good intuitive sense for adjusting conditions. With the right care, this variety performs admirably in either indoor or outdoor gardens, with an 8-9 week flowering time. Outdoors, BC Blueberry can be grown in temperate regions as long as weather does not turn before the harvesting date, around the middle of September. While this plant can be grown in any medium, soil will bring out her luscious flavors. Yields average 1.5 to 2.5 ounces (40-70g) per plant when grown indoors, or between 4 and 16 ounces (115-450g) in outdoor gardens, depending on growing conditions and vegetative times.

While three-quarters of these plants will be green, one-quarter are a phenotype that features blue tones and pink hairs. Both phenotypes have medium-thick leaves. BC Blueberry is nutrient sensitive and is a dainty eater, so growers should take care to not overfeed these plants. She can also be sensitive to overly wet conditions. At finish plants grow to 3 or 4 feet (1-1.3m), making them good for rooms with space limitations. Outdoors, they will average nearly double their indoor heights.

With some TLC, BC Blueberry rewards the hobby grower with compact sweet smelling blueberry buds that are coated with creamy resinous glands. When cured, the buds will turn blue. The effect of BC Blueberry is blissful. The high creeps into a pleasant and awake state that is very functional. Compared to many varieties, BC Blueberry's high is relatively short, but comforting and tasty.

 80I/20S

 calm, dreamy, munchies

 fruit and fuel

 55-63 days

 longtime BC Blueberry clone ♀ x unknown ♂

 100 g/plant in; 1000 g/plant out

BC God Bud

BC Bud Depot

Photo: Isabella

The memorably-named God Bud rose from underground fame in Canada's medical pot community to international acclaim when BC Bud Depot debuted her as a commercial strain in 2004. Her heavy yields and strong effect have made BC God Bud an indica worthy of praise.

BC God Bud is short, squat and dense, with plenty of silvery resin. While she does well outside in California, yielding up to 3 pounds (1.3 kg) per plant, she does not finish well as far north as British Columbia and is better for indoor cultivation in cool climates. Although BC God Bud can be hard on beginners, attentive growers will find this to be a hardy, pest resistant plant with leathery leaves and an appetite for nutrients. These plants require 8-10 weeks of flowering time to reach maturity. As the plants ripen, their dark greens turn to shades of purple, and a heady, almost high-inducing smell begins to fill the grow room, requiring some odor control precautions.

These plants stay at the shortest end of the growth spectrum, reaching only 2-3 feet (up to 1 m) in height at harvest, with a bud production that can maximize smaller spaces. While the BC God Bud is not a single-cola plant, her side branching is minimal enough to make it a good sea of green choice. Under these conditions, she can deliver a whopping 3-4 ounces (85-115 g) of compact, sparklingly resinous buds per plant.

On the toke, BC God Bud delivers a musky, tropical flavor with herbal edges and hints of lavender, berry, and pine. The high is well balanced, a slight creeper with longlasting effects, starting with a calm, pleasant feeling and increasing to a more surreal, nearly hallucinogenic buzz. She is good for general pain relief and makes a pleasant nighttime smoke. Her innerspace high flourishes in calm environments rather than loud nightclubs or high-stress social encounters. The peace of BC God Bud unfolds in the garden or at the drawing table, and in the quiet hours before bed.

1st Prize, Battle of the Bridges 2006 — A *High Times* Private Growers Competition, *USA (NY) vs Canada (Ontario)*
Named one of *High Times* Top 10 Strains of the Year, 2005
2nd prize *International Cannagraphics* 420 Cup, God Hash, 2005
1st Prize *High Times* Cannabis Cup – Best Indica, 2004

 75I/25S

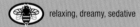 relaxing, dreamy, sedative

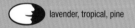 lavender, tropical, pine

 55-70 days

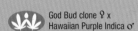 God Bud clone ♀ x Hawaiian Purple Indica ♂

 100-200g/plant

 SOG

BC Sweet God

BC Bud Depot

Photo: Isabella

BC Sweet God is a grapefruit and honey flavored indica with a noticeable likeness to her mother, the award-winning God Bud. Unlike mama, BC Sweet God has a fast finish—a short 6-7 weeks indoors. Outdoors, this indica quickness helps BC Sweet God come in before the autumn frost on the coast of British Columbia, as well in the Pacific Northwest, California, and similar latitudes.

BC Bud Depot prefers soil-based gardens, which bring out Sweet God's honey, but this plant will also perform well in a hydroponics setup, which offers faded flavors but slightly higher yields and possibly shorter flowering times. BC Sweet God takes a medium nutrient regimen and is resilient and forgiving, which, combined with her general hardiness and pest resistance, makes her a good strain for beginning gardeners.

The odor of this plant is dank while growing, requiring some protective measures. As the plants mature, their swarthy green, indica leaning foliage turns purple. This "sweet" strain is also short, reaching 4 feet (1.3 m) maximum indoors. With a little trimming, her minimal branching makes a solid sea of green plant, yielding 2.5 to 3.5 ounces (70-100 g).

Named for both her parents, BC Sweet God mixes the taste undertones of God Bud—a citrus edge, plus some pine muskiness—with Sweet Tooth's unique taste of honey. The Sweet Tooth genetics also make this plant faster and more robust in all phases of her growth. Her effects may leave tokers exclaiming "Sweet God!" as the day's cares melt away and this strain's high creeps into their limbs, bringing a calm and pleasant if slightly lethargic sense of relaxation. BC Sweet God is great for comfortable atmospheres that involve a bit of lounging, socializing, or romancing. She is also good for a nightcap, and for medicinal users seeking to alleviate pain from conditions such as arthritis.

High Times Top 10 Strain of the Year in 2006

 90I/10S

 body ease, couchlock

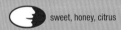 sweet, honey, citrus

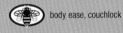 40-50 days

 BC God Bud ♀ x BC Sweet Tooth #3 ♂

 100 g/plant in SOG; 1500 g/plant out

 SOG

BC Bud Depot

In the mid-1990s, the BC Bud Depot formed as a group of connoisseurs, growers and breeders dedicated to the sacred cannabis plant. They traded clones and genetics, and created and grew premium cannabis in their homeland of coastal British Columbia. Quickly gaining a reputation as top breeders and growers in the region, they provided medical users far and wide with access to BC Bud Depot cannabis and genetics.

The BC Bud Depot remained an underground breeders' collective, not ones for the limelight, until 2004 when it finally went public with offerings of seeds and genetics on the worldwide market via the Internet. In early November, the members were in the midst of trimming up some rooms of prized God Bud in British Columbia, when *High Times* Magazine called and invited them to attend the Cannabis Cup in Amsterdam. On November 24th, 2004 at the Melkweg Hall in downtown Amsterdam, the BC Bud Depot won the Indica Cup with their modestly named entry, God Bud. This award has been followed by several others in recent years. BC Bud Depot continues to develop high quality cannabis strains for the medical community in Canada.

BC Sweet Tooth

BC Bud Depot

BC Sweet Tooth gets her name from her intense sugar on the palate, but just because she is sweet on the tongue does not mean she is dainty on the stone. The BC Sweet Tooth is a candy-coated bomb to the senses, not recommended for daytime functionality, but terrific for inducing sleep, soothing pain or indulging in languorous, mellow relaxation. The combination of medicinal-grade stone, big yields, and quick finishing time make this variety an excellent choice for impatient growers looking for a cavity-defying sweet indica.

BC Sweet Tooth finishes in 6-7 weeks, or by early to mid September in outdoor environments. This rapid schedule brings BC Sweet Tooth in before the frost in coastal British Columbia, or in locations south to the equator. Indoors, this variety can finish even faster, in as little as 40 days. BC Sweet Tooth branches moderately and can be easily manipulated to conform to either a multi-branch or sea of green gardening style.

A medium feeder that is good for beginners and connoisseurs alike, BC Sweet Tooth is a hardy plant that defends herself well against pests, but can show mold susceptibility if planted too late outdoors or raised in overly moist environments indoors. Her dense, nuggety buds look edible, and smell almost as sweet as they taste. BC Sweet Tooth's height at finish averages 3-4 feet (1 to 1.3 m) indoors or 6-8 feet (2-2.6 m) outdoors. Her average yields are 2.5-3.5 ounces (70-100 g) per plant in an indoor setup, or 4-16 ounces (115-450 g) outdoors, depending on the growing region and its conditions.

BC Sweet Tooth's syrupy buds are good medication for chronic pain, but less optimal for mixed crowds and socializing. This strain delivers a hammer to the head, and can be a day-wrecker if its effects are unanticipated. The high has a lasting effect, and can lead to couch-lock, but if a major body soothing sensation is desired, BC Sweet Tooth is a promising strain to seek out.

 90I/10S

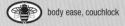 body ease, couchlock

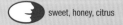 sweet, honey, citrus

 40-50 days

 BC Sweet Tooth #3 ♀ x Sweet Tooth #3 and BC Sweet Tooth IBL ♂

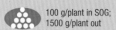 100 g/plant in SOG; 1500 g/plant out

 SOG

Big Bang

Green House Seed Company

Photo: Jan Otsen

The Big Bang is a strong, explosive indica, ideal in 5-gallon (20 L) containers, as well as for SOG or SCROG systems. This fast, compact plant forms a plump firework of a bush. Big Bang can take a lot of feeding, and will pop out some very smelly buds that can give your air filters a run for their money.

Best results are obtained in a hydroponics system, although Big Bang will also do well in soil. If this plant is allowed to grow large, its strong branching and short internode lengths will require some pruning to allow more light and air to reach the inner and lower branches. Growers should start this variety with a medium-low pH (5.6 hydro / 5.8 soil) and slowly increase to reach 6.5 at the end of flowering. EC levels depend on the system. The maximum EC should be 2.0 in hydro and 1.8 in soil. Adequate flushing should be provided. Plants in 5 gallon containers will reach 4-5 feet at harvest if grown for at least 2 weeks. Plants in smaller containers reach 2-3 feet. With no limit to root development, and ideal conditions, Big Bang can skyrocket to over 7 feet in height.

Big Bang forms small round buds with overlapping clusters of calyxes, and thick short hairs. Although her leaves are bright green, her resin dulls the color with its grayish shade. Her medium-sized leaflets tend to overlap.

Aside from describing her bursting growth, the name Big Bang also describes this strain's stone, which comes on strong and very smooth, with a semi-narcotic medicinal effect. Like a healing nova within the body, the high expands throughout the system to release tension and pain and create a soothing state. The effect is steady and longlasting. Big Bang's flavor is very intense and sweet, reminiscent of apple, rose and violet candies. Known for her medicinal properties, Big Bang is chosen by thousands of medicinal users in Holland, where it is known as "Simm-18." This strain is good as a muscle relaxer for multiple sclerosis and helps alleviate chronic pain. Big Bang will also be enjoyed recreationally by those seeking a physically relaxing effect. Big Bang won 3rd Prize in the *High Times* Cannabis Cup, 2000.

 80I/20S

 physical, muscle relaxation

 sweet, rose, violet, apple

 63 days/early Oct.

 ♀ Skunk/Northern Lights x ♂ El Nino

 up to 700 g/m² in; up to 1000 g/plant out

 SOG

Big Buddha Cheese

Big Buddha Seeds

In the UK cannabis scene, the Cheese has become one of those special and elusive strains whose name is almost synonymous with good weed. Its old school flavor and sublime effects have become a standout. Cheese was cloned only in the UK, so she remained a regional phenomenon. Based on the characteristics of her taste and high, it is believed that the Cheese clone originated from 1980s Skunk and Northern Lights lineages. Cheese clones passed between many breeders and growers, and as they circulated, several breeders attempted to capture this variety's special qualities in seed form.

Big Buddha crossed the Cheese with an Afghan male plant. Then he backcrossed to the Cheese mother for two years. Big Buddha Cheese is a unique fast flowering indica with enough sativa influences to make a truly classic smoke.

The plant exhibits more than one phenotype in her growth pattern, but all retain the important properties unique to the Cheese—the special dank, incense-like aroma, the smooth distinctive flavor and the easygoing, mellow high, which settles in calmly and is virtually without a ceiling.

Big Buddha Cheese is equally well suited for indoor and outdoor gardens. Plants are ready in 7-9 weeks when grown hydroponically, and may take an additional week when grown organically in soil or in coco. Although she can be grown in an SOG system, BBC is better as a multi-branch plant, as the internodes stretch out during flowering to produce magnificent, elegant, slender kush-like buds. During the last few weeks, bulging calyxes and glistening resin production appear when the plant is fully ripened.

Outdoors, BBC will finish in most parts of Europe well before the first frosts sets in, but the yield depends on the appropriateness of the climate. In the smell department, you have been warned! BBC starts to emanate a pong as early as the formation of the 7th node, cutting through most other smells, so Big Buddha advises taking steps to control odor both indoors and out.

 60S/40I

 uplifting, no ceiling, clear, long lasting

 old school, woodsy fresh/pungent

 49-63 days/end Oct.- beg Nov.

 ♀ Cheese x ♂ Afghani

 300 - 450 g/m² (1½ oz/ft²)

 SOG

Taste is where this variety shines. When properly dried and cured, the flavor has a special "dank" quality reminiscent of what good pot used to taste like—spicy, sweet, and kush-like. The high is very up. It can be consumed every day with little or no immunity or change in quality of the high, making BBC suitable for both recreational and medicinal use.

1rst Prize, 2006 *High Times* Cannabis Cup, Best Indica category

Who's got the Cheese!
The history of Big Buddha Seeds
Big Buddha

There are many different stories about its origin, but the consensus is that it came from some Original Seed Bank skunk seeds planted in 1988/1989 by the Exodus collective. This group of free party people was based at "the Manor," a large old home just outside of London. Exodus was taking a lead role in fighting prohibition at that time and the Manor was a persecution-free zone. It inspired loads of people to start growing, and cuttings were flying out of the door for a few years! Due to its great taste and all-prevailing stench, one of the group decided to name this plant the Cheese.

During the late 1990s I was taking photos, writing articles and interviewing breeders for *Weed World* magazine in the UK, and making good contacts within the industry. Eventually I was given some cuttings from a much respected member of the UK cannabis scene, Zorro from *Red Eye* magazine. This was when we started our backcrossing projects. We gave out a lot of our crosses to other growers as well as selecting the right progeny for breeding. Among those strains was one we named "The Kali," a really fat spicy Afghan strain. Kali was a special line, so the male from these seedlings was chosen to start the backcrossing of the clone-only Cheese.

With the ever changing fashion for different variants and flavors of cannabis, we are constantly researching and testing to find that special plant.

Blue Buddha

BC Bud Depot

Photos: Devils Harvest Krew & BC Bud Crew

Blue Buddha is a bud with an earthy spice and a clear functional high. She has a richly resonant smell that requires control and camouflage. As a moderate brancher, the Blue Buddha will cheerfully adapt to the growing path you set her on, whether that means single cola, sea of green, or multi-branching. Likewise, she will grow well indoors or out, taking 7-9 weeks indoors, or finishing in late October outside. Outdoor Blue Buddhas are calm and serene in the face of frost; they keep growing right into the days of ripeness. It is better to cut this plant down once she reaches ripeness rather than allowing her to go too long outdoors; otherwise, her flavor will begin to fade.

Blue Buddha has no gender confusion—she shows no hermaphroditic tendencies under any conditions. Her good pest resistance makes Blue Buddha a suitable choice for the novice gardener as well as the pro. While ripening, this plant truly reeks. Her fast finishing time produces satisfyingly chunky and dense buds with a smell that fades to subtle diesel perfume, tinges of blue coloration, and a fuzzy carpeting of resin that is sure to please.

The Blue Buddha flavor is velvety deep, with dank skunkiness and a slightly sweet, blueberry creaminess. The high mixes a little sativa influence with a heavy Afghani stone. At first it lifts you up, making you feel a little encouraged about just about everything, then it wraps you in a blanket of nice fogginess. Although the first wave is a spurt of energy, this feeling shifts into a moderately long lasting couchlock that is awake, but dreamy. Blue Buddha is good for enhancing a contemplative mood in which to indulge the imagination, reflection and artistic impulses.

 75I/25S

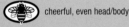 cheerful, even head/body

 spicy, whisky, fuel

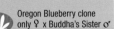 65 days

 Oregon Blueberry clone only ♀ x Buddha's Sister ♂

 100 g/plant in; 1500 g/plant out

 SOG

The History of Blue Buddha
By BC Bud Depot

Special thanks to MoonShineMan and the late Direwulfe (9/5/1954-11/12/2006)

In the fall of 1985 or 1986, my brother was doing a little Pacific Coast trip, mainly hanging out in Northern California and Oregon. He stopped at a state park somewhere among the redwoods to take a leak and catch a few winks of sleep. He hooked up there with a few old heads who were smoking in the woods. They were puffing this Blueberry. He asked them if he could buy a sack or a nug because it was so flavorful and it ripped him to the core. The fella said, "Sorry bro, don't got any bud, but I do have some clones I'm taking to a friend. I'll sell you a couple of those." So my brother bought three rooted clones from these guys in the woods.

Around 1990, when I turned 18, I had my own room above the store where I worked. My brother decided that it would be a good place to grow some Blueberry. He came over one day and set up a 1000-watt HPS light and ten Blueberries and said to get at it … and not to kill them! That started our path to the Blue Buddha. We called the first strain of Blueberry "Ol' Blue" just because she was so old. When my brother originally bought her, she was called Oregon Blueberry. If I was on an island and could only have one strain, it would be her. She was Blue Buddha's mother.

Blue Buddha's father comes from Soma originally. I can say that in all the years I've grown from seed, I have never seen a male with such amazing qualities as this fella. Huge pollen sacs that drop teaspoon-sized loads of pollen, very vigorous growth with no stress, nicely spaced nodes, great stem thickness, actual visible crystals and the strongest funk of any plant in veg I have had. This male smelled stronger than my Maple Leaf, more like Maple Leaf and a cargo truck filled with dead skunks. Soma's genetics are so good that I can't help wanting to spread them around. What better way than by crossing his super-male with all of my specially selected ladies, creating a new line of super hybrids. Blue Buddha is one of the first, and we think you will be pleased with the results of our selection.

Blue Cheese

Big Buddha Seeds

 80I/20S

 physical, muscle relaxation

 sweet, rose, violet, apple

 63 days/early Oct.

 ♀ Skunk/Northern Lights x ♂ El Nino

 up to 700 g/m2 in; up to 1000 g/plant out

 SOG

Blue Cheese was created by crossing a set of Blueberry males, acquired from several different breeders, with Big Buddha Cheese, the backbone of many of Big Buddha's breeding projects (*see Big Buddha Cheese*). The resulting seeds were grown out and a male was selected from 40 different Blueberry x Cheese male contestants, becoming the proud papa of this pungent strain. The selected Blueberry Cheese male was then crossed once again with a Big Buddha Cheese female, making this hybrid a mostly cheese plant with a hint of blueberry.

Blue Cheese has round swirls of compact flowers that develop distinctly purple hues near the finish. The close internodes of this plant make it highly suitable for sea of green growing. Indoor plants in SOG mature in 8-10 weeks. She produces a huge main cola indoors or out, with respectable additions to the yield from the controlled side branching. In the last two weeks, this strain shows a real burst of resin and starts to deliver a truly funky smell. Outdoors, this strain finishes around Halloween.

Blue Cheese's flavor has a soft fruity kiss of blueberry that fans of the fruit will appreciate, anchored in a strong underlying flavor that is unmistakably Cheese—slightly funky and dank with a woodsy edge. The combined taste is musky and spicy with a sweet cotton candy note and a hint of berries on the exhale. While the yield is not as abundant as some commercial strains selected for their pumped-up buds, growers in search of connoisseur flavors will find the yield to be generous when compared to other varieties in this category.

The biggest pleasure of the Blue Cheese is its high, which comes on smooth and easy, and stays very functional while creating a feeling of great euphoria and an opening into the awareness of possibility, bringing with it the potential to face the day with a positive outlook. This high opens the mind by relaxing the body. It's a comforting, balanced vibe that can take a nice long walk, or sit by the fire at home.

Brainstorm Haze

Delta-9 Labs

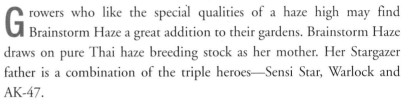

 mostly sativa

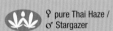 social, creative

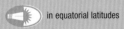 sweet, fresh

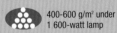 70-84 days

 ♀ pure Thai Haze / ♂ Stargazer

 400-600 g/m² under 1 600-watt lamp

 in equatorial latitudes

Growers who like the special qualities of a haze high may find Brainstorm Haze a great addition to their gardens. Brainstorm Haze draws on pure Thai haze breeding stock as her mother. Her Stargazer father is a combination of the triple heroes—Sensi Star, Warlock and AK-47.

Brainstorm Haze shows its haze heritage in its stretchy growth and long flowering cycle. The average flowering time for Brainstorm Haze is 10-12 weeks, with significant stretching in the first 2 weeks. However, as it begins to mature, it may break the stereotype of the haze grow—once the buds start to fill in, the plant stops growing any taller. It looks like a tree with many branches and leaves rather than a bush. The leaves are thin, but not as elongated as many strong sativa leaves.

Brainstorm's parentage may also lead one to expect light airy buds, another haze characteristic, but here again, this plant breaks with the pattern. For the first 5-8 weeks, the Brainstorm buds will remain relatively fluffy, but waiting for full maturity is key, as they begin to swell and tighten into hard dense buds during the last 3 weeks of flowering.

The flowering time lessens and the yield improves when Brainstorm Haze is grown using hydroponic methods. Neem oil can be a gardener's best defense against pests and disease, and regular treatments will help keep Brainstorm Haze a happy camper in the grow room.

Outdoors, this variety will do well in warm climates in the southern equatorial latitudes. Indoors and out, the Brainstorm Haze is a tropical beauty, always more at home in the heat than in a cooler setting.

While haze strains take some gardening skill and patience, many growers undertake the slightly higher maintenance for the rewards—a very clear-headed and uplifting high with a fresh, sweet aroma and flavor. Haze's fruity floral fragrance is perhaps as distinctive and recognizable as lavender is in the larger herbal family. The Brainstorm Haze buzz is a creeper, taking about 10 minutes to reach an even and motivating high that keeps the creativity and conversation flowing. Brainstorm offers a comfortable high you can ease into rather than the punch of intensity that some people find startling or paranoia-inducing. The soft shift combined with the mental clarity and peaceful soul quality of this variety make it conducive to sociability and moments of thoughtful reflection.

Delta-9's Grow Tips on Fertilizing

In our growing stage nursery we like to alternate between a high nutrient tea mixture and a pure water supply in our reservoir. Often, we top-dress many of our mother plants with a well-balanced guano powder to maintain the extra food required for such large plants. The fresh, clean water refreshes the plants and helps break down the guano powder. This allows any residual nutrients to break loose, and get smoothly absorbed by the root system before the next feeding.

Burmese Kush

TH Seeds

 60I/40S

 mellow, creeper

 sweet, conifer

 50-56 days

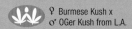 ♀ Burmese Kush x ♂ OGer Kush from L.A.

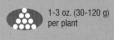 1-3 oz. (30-120 g) per plant

 SOG

Burmese Kush draws from old-world genetics, a dark green sativa-indica hybrid from Burma that has a quick finishing time. This plant has been married to one of the old school California strains—a TH Seeds specialty. Although she is almost half sativa, this hybrid stays quite small and exhibits hardly any branching. These qualities make the Burmese Kush perfect for the sea of green gardening method.

TH Seeds feeds this plant organic bio dynamic food from Botanicare, but she responds very well to all fertilizers. Outdoors she is a bit of a slow starter. TH Seeds recommends pre-flowering for best results. Despite the slow start, she grows very quickly once established, and can finish in 7 to 8 weeks, making her one of TH Seed's fastest strains.

This compact mama reaches about 1 foot (30 cm) during typical vegging and triples to around 3 feet (100 cm) at the end of flowering. When grown in a sea of green, plants usually yield around an ounce (25-35 g) each. Plants grown in 1-gallon containers will deliver closer to 2 ounces (35-60 g), while those grown in 5-gallon buckets can yield up to 125 g per plant.

Burmese Kush develops from top to bottom, with slight lower branching appearing late in maturation. She produces tight buds with very small dense trichomes. The buds' color is a classic dark Kush green. The leaves are thin and flat. The buds begin to blow out at two weeks of flowering, forming dense and resin-coated nuggets. While she thrives in high heat conditions, Burmese Kush exhibits a vulnerability to powdery mildew if conditions are overly humid or wet.

The BK buzz is a creeper, but when it arrives, the feeling is calming and brings a centered sensation rather than a big gong to the head. It is good for those that prefer a mellow high instead of a heart-racing speedy sensation. Her aroma and flavor is decidedly pine, with a subtle sweetness that lingers pleasantly on the tongue. This is not your pot for jet-setting, but for relaxing and enjoying a leisurely meal once you've arrived at your destination. Its genetic makeup suggests medical applications for pain relief and appetite enhancement.

45

Casey Jones

Head Seeds

Photo: Ms. Grateful

Casey Jones combines an excellent sativa mother, a Trainwreck x Thai, with an outstanding male from Rezdog's Sour Diesel v3 line. The mother originated from Billy Goat Seed's Oriental Express cross. She has a very sweet flavor, and a heady trancendent high.

Adding Diesel to Trainwreck suggested the name Casey Jones, engineer of the most famous train wreck of all time. The sativa-dominant Casey Jones strain has an amazing high. The plant varies slightly in structure, from Thai foxtails to Diesel plumes. It retains the short ripening time of the Oriental Express mother, finishing in about 8 weeks. Casey Jones is not overly picky, suiting the novice grower as well as the sweet-toothed connoisseur.

This variety multi-branches well, especially when trained. She prefers moderate feeding and grows to a final height of 30-40 inches when forced at 12-16 inches. When plants are grown short with a single cola (SOG style), they yield an average of $^1/_3$ to $^1/_2$ ounce (10-14 g). Grown large and trained, plants could yield up to 3.5 ounces (100 g) each.

The buds form like towers of calyxes, tight but clustered, creating a looser cola, with colorful pistils that vary from orange to pink. The leaves have thin blades and stems may purple late in the flowering phase.

The Casey Jones flavor is a combination of the confection-like sweet Oriental Express and the citric sour of the Diesel. The high can be felt almost immediately and lasts about an hour and a half. This strain has an "up" effect with a vividly trippy, thought provoking quality that can lead to mental wandering. Under its effects, one may feel a stronger sense of connectedness to self and others. It is good for creative activities that can benefit from an introspective mood and don't require intense right brain focus. It is less than ideal if you need to make plans, balance your checkbook or do other very linear activities. Go fly a kite, watch a movie, hike around in the outdoors, or engage in a little painting or other interpretive activity when indulging in Casey Jones. Do not drive a train!

 80S/20I

 up, trippy

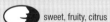 sweet, fruity, citrus

 56-63 days

 ♀ Trainwreck x Thai from Billygoat Seeds x ♂ East Coast Sour Diesel v3 from Reservoir Seeds

 average 25-30 g/plant

Chrystal

Nirvana Seed Bank

Chrystal is a child of celebrity parents, destined for her own renown. The Chrystal mother derives from the legendary White Widow strain. White Widow set the standard for "White" strains. Nirvana's White Widow is a tall plant with delicate arms and moderately compact copiously resinous buds.

To breed Chrystal, Nirvana backcrossed White Widow with famed daddy Northern Lights. This Northern Lights leans to the sativa side with a powerful, energetic, and very social buzz.

As would be expected, this marriage produced a plant with a lot of good genetics. Chrystal is a fine indoor plant, whether the garden is a soil or hydro system. Soil-based gardens bring out more complex flavors and aromas, while hydro setups deliver more commercial-style buds that are compact and easy to trim, but diminish this plant in the smell department.

This F1 hybrid grows quite aggressively, so growth should be controlled. Toward the end of flowering, all branches have to be staked and supported. Fortunately, the high bud-to-leaf ratio from her Northern Lights father makes Chrystal a pretty easy plant to manicure. When placed into flowering at 16 inches (40 cm), Chrystal can easily reach 3 feet (1 m) at maturity. Her growth structure makes sea of green an efficient choice, although Nirvana has seen greenhouse gardens where Chrystal was grown as a multi-branched plant. These greenhouse ladies reach 6 feet (2 m) in height and yield 750 grams of quality grass per plant.

Chrystal's sticky buds have noticeable kerosene overtones—a clean but pungent lawn-mower whiff. The effects are quick hitting, producing an all-around high that can be felt in both body and mind. In other words, the stone reflects the balance, acceleration, and power of Chrystal's parentage. Chrystal took first place in the Dutch Highlife Cup, 2002.

 I S 60I/40S

 fast, head/body

 kerosene

 56-70 days/ Sept.-Oct.

 ♀ White Widow x ♂ Northern Lights backcross

 375-475/m² in SOG

 greenhouse

 SOG

Cinderella 99 x Panama Red

Wally Duck

The name of this variety leads you right to the parentage. The mother, Panama Red, is a pure sativa strain from South America. The father, Cinderella 99, is a fast maturing, resiny sativa strain originating with the Brothers Grimm in Holland. Cindy 99 is a cross from a Jack Herer bag seed that was "cubed" to create Cinderella 99 (see the story in *The Big Book of Buds 2*).

For this cross, Wally Duck has bred Cinderella 99 specifically for taste. He discovered among several grows that some Cindy 99s had an increased pineapple flavor. In the fifth cross of these pineapple types, he added the Panama Red to produce this very resiny, pineapple-smelling plant. In addition to flavor, the Cindy father was selected for fast maturation and high resin content, while the Panama Red mother was chosen for the trippy, euphoric effects. Together, these two sativa strains yield a pure sativa whose high and taste really shines when grown in an acclimated outdoor climate.

Wally Duck prefers to grow cannabis outside in his tropics location, which is the favored home of pure sativas. C99 x PR was happy to finish on sub-equatorial days (no longer than 13 hours) without signs of revegging. Outdoors, sativas need a climate that won't frost too early in the season. This variety is right at home in the heat—in an outdoor test patch, C99 x PR was dealt a very steamy season and showed no signs of trouble, also tolerating some gaps in watering. Because of its hardiness and willingness to put up with some neglect and abuse, this plant is suitable for a beginning outdoor gardener who is in the 40° latitude region.

Indoors, this variety is more suitable for a grower who has a little experience. Optimum indoor ripeness takes 70 days from forcing at a 12/12 cycle. C99 x PR does well in a screen of green (SCROG), where branches can be trained for maximum yield. A soil medium adds depth to this strain's flavor, but she has also done well in hydro methods.

 100% sativa

 talkative, mentally stimulating

 spicy, pineapple

 70 days

 ♀ Panama Red x ♂ Cinderella 99

 30 g/plant in; 4-8 oz./plant out

 in equatorial regions

SOG

Given a chance, this plant can get quite large, with several long main colas. With a minimum vegetative time, outdoor plants reach 5 feet and yield between 4 and 8 ounces per plant. Indoors with minimum vegetative times, the plants yield around 1 ounce (30 grams) each, which increases if they are vegged longer and allowed ample room for the subsequent increase in size.

When allowed to progress without much manipulation or pruning, this plant becomes more round and bushlike than the classic marijuana profile. C99 x PR buds are compact and stacked, but not super chunky. Outdoors they look like foxtails, thick and long, surrounded by some typically slender sativa foliage.

This strain tastes like pineapple, with a pleasant spiciness and a hint of pepper in the exhale. The high is filled with the sweet effects of sativa. The high comes on fast—a talkative, awake, idea-liberating buzz with a trippy edge. Once your thoughts are tingling and fully stimulated, C99 x PR is good for lengthy chats with your favorite conversation partners. It may be good for bouncing around some interesting ideas, but focused work or planning is best saved for later.

D-Line (aka Chocolope)

DNA Genetics

With D-Line, DNA Genetics continues their project of creating tasty short-flowering sativas and reviving the classic features of old school Thai stick. The strain's father, Cannalope, is a sativa line backcrossed for fast finishing. DNA refined this feature still further, then crossed a Cannalope male with an Original Chocolate Thai female. Tasting is believing: the result retains the special flavors and effects of the OG Chocolate Thai, and lives up to the nickname Chocolope in flavor as well as genetics. It brings back a chocolate edge that was more common among good weed of the 1980s, mixed with the fruity sweetness of the Cannalope.

D-Line is a branchy near-pure sativa that will take over your garden if you let her. This plant needs some space to spread out her long branches. Hydro, coco beds, NFT, it's all good: the Chocolope likes all mediums, although she remains untested outdoors.

DNA vegetates the D-Line for 3-4 weeks and then forces flowering, preferring to raise fewer plants to larger sizes. D-Line is a happy eater and can be pushed when it comes to nutrients, although DNA recommends sticking to the organics for the best quality. Using this combination of fewer but bigger plants and organic nutrients, DNA reports an average yield of 100 grams (3.5 oz.) per plant. If you want to avoid a 3-4 week vegetative period and plant 20-25 plants per square meter in a more sea of green style, yields can reach 400-600 grams (14-21 oz.) per square meter. On the whole, D-Line is much easier to grow than her Chocolate Thai ancestors. "Give her love," says DNA, "and she will yield for you."

The D-Line still delivers traits many growers sought from the classic Thai strains—choco-smokey flavor and a dreamy high with a strong mental shift. If you are trying to alleviate anxiety, nervousness, or lack of appetite, the Chocolope is your strain. However, smokers who are sensitive to paranoia or psychedelic effects might approach this variety with caution. Even experienced smokers sometimes report unusually comic situations due to the "high school" like stone of the D-Line. Some consider this advice a recommendation: the chocolatey 1980s high is a euphoric and trippy blast from the not-so-distant past that can spice up any weekend.

 95S/5I

 old school

 chocolatey

 63-70 days

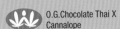 O.G.Chocolate Thai X Cannalope

 100 g/plant

 SOG

Thai Stick

Ed Rosenthal Super Bud

Sensi Seed Bank

 65I/35S

 creative, light-hearted

 tropical, fruit salad

 55-65 days/Nov. 1

 Afghanis, North Indian, Thai, African, Mexican, Jamaican

 up to 500g/m² in; up to 135g/plant in/ up to 500g/plant out

 SOG

Sensi Seed Bank has released this elite strain in honor of Ed Rosenthal, the undisputed heavyweight champion of growing gurus. Literally decades in the making, this hybrid achieves a superb layering of traits from both the indica and sativa ends of the cannabis spectrum. This variety was refined from the "Potent Evolved Hybrid" project, where pure Afghani cultivars and equatorial sativa strains were interbred over many years, and their offspring selected for potency and yield at every step. The blend of tropical genes in ER Super Bud's background is especially wide-ranging, representing sativas from all around the equatorial zone—Africa, South East Asia, Central America and the Caribbean.

Ed Rosenthal Super Bud thrives outdoors in hot climates, and should be grown indoors in temperate or cold regions like Holland. Any medium is fine, and plants enjoy standard to generous fertilizer feedings. ER Super Bud is very manageable as she grows, with a surprisingly uniform growth pattern given her diverse heritage. This strain is suitable for sea of green; alternatively, both her indica and sativa phenotypes can be grown into excellent multi-stem plants.

Succulent flower formation is the Super Bud strain's distinguishing feature. All females exhibit flower structures bursting with indica density, made even fatter by the running sativa tendency. The result is buds that swell upwards and outwards to crazy sizes and sport a stupendous covering of full-sized resin glands. ER buds also have a unique pistil formation—the oversized antennae sprouting from each calyx are covered with a visible fuzz of tiny hairs, giving them a 'woolly' appearance. Different individuals show extra sativa or indica influence through subtle variations in the development and structure of their resin-soaked buds. The sativa-leaning females make particularly good multi-stem plants and produce huge oval calyxes which spiral into crooked bud-pyramids large enough to bend branches.

The indica phenotype's flowers are distinct and impressive, building into voluptuous columns of snowy bud with main colas as thick as an arm. In other respects, phenotype variation is small, with a majority of plants flowering at the same speed and increasing their height by about 150%. A small proportion will show a jump at the onset of blooming, which first widens the gaps between internodes and later gives an even greater yield potential.

All plants from this strain are sweet smelling and taste of pineapple punch. As for the stone—get ready for an immediate body flush, a bright physical glow that's not given to lethargy. Later, a cerebral high creeps up, subtle at first, yet longer lasting than the body effect. Ed Rosenthal Super Bud is sweetly relaxing, leaving plenty of energy for conversation and socializing with friends. Medicinally, this might be a good variety for chronic body pain and the blues that come with it.

Ed Rosenthal Super Bud
Sensi Seed Bank

From the inception of the modern cannabis revolution, Ed Rosenthal has been at the heart of the movement, a committed and fearless campaigner for truth, justice and sanity, which is to say, an end to prohibition.

If you've ever grown ganja, it's a safe bet that Ed has helped you out in a big way, whether directly or indirectly. He's taught generations of growers about the science and art of cannabis cultivation, and helped them discover their green thumb as well as the joys and potential for personal enrichment that this hobby can awaken.

As the brain behind the *Ask Ed* columns in *Cannabis Culture* and *High Times,* and the author of a veritable library of cannabis books that cover every topic from growing to law reform, Ed Rosenthal has done more than anyone we know to spread accurate, no-nonsense information on the world's most delightful crop.

It's no exaggeration to say that Ed Rosenthal Super Bud has been decades in the making. Sharp-eyed cannabis historians and collectors of old seed catalogues might have seen the single printed reference to the breeding

program that eventually led to the Super Bud strain. In 1989, this Ed-affiliated strain was called Ed's Potent Evolved Hybrid Type 1 (PEHT), when it was briefly offered in a limited edition of 1500 seeds. It sold out very quickly and was never commercially offered again. Around this time, there was a big shift toward indoor cultivation and few growers had the time or space for experimental crossings. Sensi Seed Bank's releases in the following years were geared toward this new indoor trend, featuring stabilized F1 hybrids—strains that could be relied upon for predictable behavior.

As the years passed, and Sensi's breeding-stock expanded into a truly comprehensive collection of traditional cultivars and legendary hybrids, their breeders found plenty of fascinating new possibilities

to explore, and the PEHT program continued quietly in the background. With occasional infusions of promising new genetic material and dozens more generations of crossing and selection for yield and resin production, the program yielded several rarefied plants which proved to be valuable intermediate parents in complex hybrids.

A desirably heavy, sticky form began to dominate the later PEHT generations. Breeders focused on stabilizing the finer points of the emerging strain. Unique flower structures and flavors discovered in the program were successfully reproduced as recurring traits and the ER seed strain neared completion. By this time, near the end of the 1990s, Holland's tolerance for cannabis was in sharp decline, and professional breeding became much more difficult, as the large crops of test seedlings required for rigorous selection were no longer possible.

As a result, the small amount of refinement required before releasing ER in its final distinct form took many years longer than expected, making this hybrid the longest single project in the Sensi Seed Bank collection. Sensi feels this world-class strain shows the years of work and care invested in its development. This gourmet hybrid promises to be a special addition to any serious aficionado's garden.

F-13

DJ Short

 60S/40I

 awake, refreshing, dreamy

 sweet, musky

 55-65 days/late Sept.

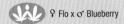 ♀ Flo x ♂ Blueberry

 75-150 g/m²

F-13 is a top-quality connoisseur variety developed with the indoor soil grower in mind. Even so, it adapts well to hydroponic systems, performing especially well in organic-based aquaponic or aeroponic setups. It has also been tested in outdoor gardens at 45° north latitude, where it performed well.

The parents of F-13 are a dynamic duo from DJ Short's Delta-9 Blue Collection. The mother strain, Flo, is an early maturing sativa/indica hybrid with the unique ability to produce a continuous harvest of tight spear-shaped buds. Her buzz is energetic and extremely clearheaded, a true "wake and bake" pot with a flowery smell and fruity undertones in the flavor. The Blueberry father is a superstar of connoisseur cannabis known for its cool blue hues and signature blueberry taste, along with its long lasting, euphoric high.

In F-13, this combination results is a slightly sativa-dominant hybrid that branches into a medium-sized, bushy plant, especially when topped. Her thin, sativa-like leaves are dark green, often developing red and lavender hues as she matures. F-13 thrives on organic nutrients with plenty of good worm castings and bat guano. Keep other feeding light, especially where nitrogen is concerned.

F-13 finishes in approximately 8-9 weeks indoors with a yield between 1-2 ounces (25-50 g) per square foot when the light input is at least 50 watts per square foot. Another measure of expected yield is 1 gram per watt of light when conditions are optimal. In outdoor grows, harvest is in late September to mid or late October depending on the latitude.

This hybrid forms tight, elongated spear- or spade-shaped buds that release a sweet musky odor while growing. The high is a creeper that takes between 20 minutes to an hour to reach its peak. The refreshing quality of the high is comfortable yet awake, making it well suited to social situations. F-13 is a lucid and truly enjoyable daytime smoke that tapers off into a dreamy feeling. Overall this variety is very motivational when used in moderation. It retains the flavors of fruit and flower that are signatures of DJ's Blue strains, making it a good choice for any flavor connoisseur.

First Lady

Sensi Seed Bank

First Lady is a highly resinous all-indica strain typically grown indoors with lights. She is excellent in a SOG setup, either in her natural shape or when pruned to 2-4 stems. First Lady's growth is compact and vigorous, with thick sturdy stems, broad leaves, and a strong symmetry that helps the buds soak up plenty of light. Branches tend to push up and out; lower lateral branches should be pruned away if they start to compete for space. This indica enjoys generous nutrient feedings in the second half of flowering—up to the full dose recommended by the manufacturer. First Lady finishes indoors in an average of 45-50 days and outdoors by early October.

The buds are classic Afghani—solid clusters at every bract and internode that form tight round nuggets crowning a collar of fat, dark green leaves. Plants exposed to cool breezes have a tendency to develop purple tones in the calyxes and even more pronounced in the foliage. Calyxes at the apex of terminal buds may start to build on top of each other after the lower part of the plant is mature, leading to multi-peaked tops. The most weight is produced on the unpruned main stem or on topped stems that have been properly vegetated.

The overall shape of the plant is more spruce than conifer; it has a central column of bud as its main feature rather than a more umbrella-like canopy. Like many indicas, the First Lady increases 50-100% from its vegetative height during flowering. Its size is manageable in an indoor setup, and can be controlled in a range from a minimal 1$\frac{1}{4}$ feet (40 cm) to a max 4.3 feet (130 cm) when vegged for 4-6 weeks. When allowed to vegetate to a larger size, this plant averages 100 grams per plant indoors.

First Lady is a naturally tough robust plant with a healthy resilience to pests or other inhospitable garden conditions. This robustness combined with the fast finish makes it satisfying for beginners. If irrigated well, she can withstand heat, and stress from fluctua-

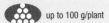 100% indica

 mellow, relaxing

 spicy/earthy

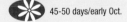 45-50 days/early Oct.

 ♀ Afghani T x ♂ Ortega

 up to 100 g/plant

 below 45° N latitude

tions in temperature from day to night; however, this Afghani native appreciates a dry atmosphere, especially in the later part of flowering. The easiest mistake with this variety might be overwatering or creating an overly humid atmosphere. First Lady's resilient genetics also make her a good candidate for cloning.

First Lady's flavor is spicy with some acridity and earthiness, and a gentle honey undertone. The immediate stoney hit segues into a long lasting body-centered buzz. This warm, happy high encourages an affinity and contentment with one's surroundings and can greatly enhance sensual pleasures, whether they be food, music or physical contact. While functional, this high is better for lounging on a weekend than motivating oneself to get up and out. It is a good appetite stimulator and muscle relaxer and might be good for a camping weekend.

First Lady

When seeds of exotic, stocky, hash-making strains from Afghanistan, Pakistan and northern India were first introduced to the west a generation ago, they changed the face of indoor growing and made names like Kandahar and Mazar-i-Sharif part of the cannabis lexicon. Many growers are interested in strains that preserve the original Indica characteristics, before they were mixed with today's diverse, global cannabis gene-pool. So there's always a good reason to release a back-to-basics Afghani. The challenge was to release one that could stand alongside Afghani #1 and Maple Leaf Indica. First Lady exemplifies the qualities of the original Indica females whose genes are now carried in hundreds of hybrid strains. Also, when flowered alongside other strains, these Afghani girls should be the first of your ladies to finish.

Fruit of the Gods

Delta-9 Labs

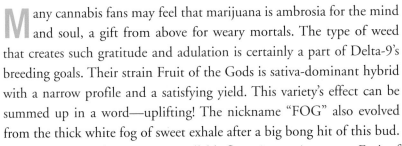

 mostly sativa

 uplifting

 fruity, floral

 66-77 days

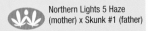 Northern Lights 5 Haze (mother) x Skunk #1 (father)

 30-50 g/plant at 3 ft.

 SOG

Many cannabis fans may feel that marijuana is ambrosia for the mind and soul, a gift from above for weary mortals. The type of weed that creates such gratitude and adulation is certainly a part of Delta-9's breeding goals. Their strain Fruit of the Gods is sativa-dominant hybrid with a narrow profile and a satisfying yield. This variety's effect can be summed up in a word—uplifting! The nickname "FOG" also evolved from the thick white fog of sweet exhale after a big bong hit of this bud.

When grown indoors in a controllable flowering environment, Fruit of the Gods takes $9^1/_2$ to 11 weeks to finish, depending on whether she is grown in soil or using hydro methods. This variety can also be grown outdoors in many regions. Warmer outdoor climates will result in yields that are 25-50% higher than indoor or temperate grows. Delta-9 uses neem oil for pest control with this strain, although FOG is naturally quite bug-resistant, and resilient under many growing conditions.

When Delta-9 grows out their strains, they use soil exclusively, with organic nutrients. However, FOG will do well in any indoor system, and may even be more prodigious and ripen in slightly less time with a hydroponic setup. While her height will depend on the length of the vegetative period, FOG is a moderate grower. She starts stretching out a bit in the first two weeks of flowering, and doubles in height by week three. These plants create many long side branches that hug the main stem. Her leaves are short and wide, like the leaves on her Skunk #1 poppa. They are narrower than a typical sativa leaf, so the end result is a broad elongated leaf blade. Overall, FOG looks like a small bushy plant with many branches close to the main stem. Even when kept short and grown in small spaces, Fruit Of the Gods produces well: in an average-sized room with proper ventilation and lighting, FOG will give you a minimum of 30-50 grams per 3 ft. (1 m) plant.

The "fruits" of this strain are light and airy as they fill in during the first 5 to 8 weeks.

Then in the last 3 weeks they harden. Their calyxes swell up and become tight, creating small but very dense buds. FOG tastes sweet, with a hazy, floral perfume that lingers throughout the room in the thick white cloud of its exhale. The FOG high is clear-headed and uplifting. As such it is very functional and easy to maintain even during a period of work or socializing. As soon as the buzz reaches your head, it creates a momentum to get things done, and motivate with friends or focus on a project.

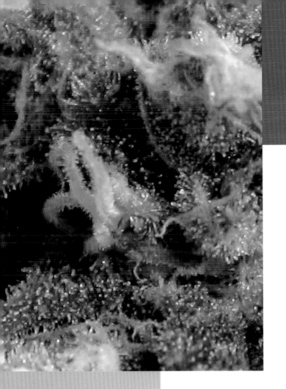

Fruity Thai

Ceres Seeds

F ruity Thai is the urban crop with a tropical twist, a blend of sweet Thai sativa with a dense and resinous indica. The combination creates a fresh and sweet "retro" Thai flavor and a clear sativa-style high, combined with a very good, very resinous indica yield. Ceres Seeds searched for a hybrid with sativa properties when it came to flavor and effect, as well as the best growing traits of a premium indica, like a shorter flowering time, sticky buds, and of course a heavy crop. They crossed a gorgeous classic Thai back-and-forth with a specially selected stock indica. Playing on the notion that sativas get you "high" and indicas get you "stoned," Ceres bills the resulting strain as "the indica that gets you Thai high!"

Indoors, Fruity Thai delivers both quality and quantity. This variety also produces amazing results in the greenhouse. While flowering, Fruity Thai looks much like a sativa plant, with a single large main cola and long, thinner branches around the base. Like a pure sativa, she still stretches a little at the start. As she matures, her buds build up from tight clusters of flowers into compact pointy cones that weigh in at comfortable yields of one gram per watt of light. Fruity Thai plants take only 8-9 weeks to mature.

Fruity Thai buds are covered with thousands of tiny, but clear, THC crystals, making them look like a starry night against a dark green sky. Besides her glittering and weighty harvest, the most notable features of this variety are her scent and flavor. Fruity Thai produces little odor while flowering, but once the buds are ripe, they release a noticeable fresh and fruity scent. The taste has overtones of lemon and melon. The effect of Fruity Thai is a comfortable, dreamy, but functional high. The vibe is sensual and communicative, happy and playful.

Fruity Thai took home Second Place in the indica category at the 2006 *High Times* Cannabis Cup, and proved a popular party favor at the Grass-A-Matazz Jazz 'n' Grass party afterwards, sponsored in part by Ceres Seeds.

 50S/50I

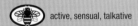 active, sensual, talkative

 lemon, melon

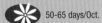 50-65 days/Oct.

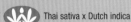 Thai sativa x Dutch indica

 1 g/w of lights
400 g/plant out

 in/out greenhouse

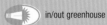 SOG

Ceres Seeds

Ceres Seeds is a 100% homegrown Dutch seed company. Its history goes back to 1988 when its owners started their first seeds and cuttings. One of the founders became a bit of an urban legend when he went to buy cuttings and growing supplies at Positronics—with his grandmother! The Ceres Seeds guys were learning the ropes back then. In the early 1990s, they worked for the old, infamous Dreadlock Coffeeshop, as well as reputable seed companies like the Sensi Seed Bank, where they learned how to produce and cross good, healthy plants, and how to know good cannabis when they saw it.

Ceres' original seeds came from the imported Jamaican, Thai, and Colombian weed that formed the stock of many coffeeshops in Amsterdam before the modern varieties took over. With a little help from their friends throughout the Dutch cannabis industry, Ceres Seeds also acquired some indica-dominant varieties that had been in already Holland for many generations.

In the late 1990s, seed companies started popping up everywhere. The guys at Ceres Seeds were surprised that many of these companies were making F2 varieties (hybrids crossed with hybrids). They decided get serious and jump in the game, making their own varieties. They approached breeding with the simple philosophy of simple, reliable and 100% stable strains. They started with landrace genetics that were available from Sensi, plus the good indica seeds they had collected over the years in Holland. "Then," says Ceres, "we remembered the old sativa seeds from all those baggies of weed we had smoked ten or fifteen years earlier. We started testing, growing, experimenting, selecting and reproducing using the best seeds from all our collections." In 1999 they made the big step and started Ceres Seeds. They took the name from Ceres, the Roman goddess of agriculture and motherly love. Her name derives from the Proto-Indo-European root "ker," meaning "to grow," which is also the root for the words "create" and "increase."

Ceres' first F1 variety, White Smurf, was introduced in 2000. With the invaluable help of the well-known "Smurf" name from an established local coffeeshop, this variety won two awards at the *High Times* Cannabis Cup that year. This gave Ceres the encouragement they needed. They continued to work on their prize stock and added other varieties such as Northern Lights x Skunk #1, Ceres Kush, and White Indica to their offerings.

Hempshopper, a great hemp and cannabis gift shop that opened its doors on the Nieuwezijds Voorburgwal in 2004, is home to Ceres Seeds in Amsterdam. From here, Ceres Seeds helped produce the first Grass-A-Matazz in 2005. The Grass-A-Matazz is a Jazz 'n Grass party, featuring the legendary John Sinclair. It is held during the annual *High Times* Cannabis Cup, and represents the blues and jazz roots in our cannabis history. At the first party, Ceres presented their new variety Fruity Thai (see preceding page). The following year, this strain won Second Prize at the Cannabis Cup in the indica category.

G-13 Diesel

Head Seeds

 60I/40S

 mellow body stone

 citrus, diesel

 58-65 days

 ♀ G-13 x G-13 backcross x ♂ East Coast Sour Diesel v3 from Reservoir Seeds

 30-35 g/plant

Head Seeds acquired the G-13 through a Pacific Northwest connection who supplied cuttings. Here, the potent indica has been mated with a Diesel, one of the popular sativa-dominant strains noted for a strong stone, and an aroma of grapefruit rind edging toward truck fuel. Diesel hybrids are popular in Amsterdam's coffeshops due to their attractive combination of sativa and indica traits in the high.

G-13 Diesel is a hardy, easy-growing plant that prefers heavy to moderate feeding. This plant multi-branches well, but is very tractable for growers who prefer a compact, bush-like profile. Plants that begin flowering at 12 to 16 inches will grow moderately, not quite doubling in height to finish around 22 inches. When G-13 Diesel is grown small with a single cola, she yields 7 to 10 grams per plant. When grown large and trained, she could easily yield a pound or more.

This strain's leaves maintain a deep green up until the last week or so of flowering; some plants take on purple tones in the stems and leaves late in their flowering cycle. G-13 Diesel buds are typical in shape: broad at the base and narrow at the tip, with pistils ranging from reddish brown to dark pink. The buds are fairly compact, but not dense enough to promote mold. The diesel aroma announces itself during the vegetative phase and becomes very strong late in flowering, requiring some attention to odor control. The smoke's flavor is sweet and skunky with unpredictable notes of citrus and diesel.

This hybrid's high starts in the head, with a cerebral flight of ideas, but quickly works its way into the body for a long lasting stone. In many respects, G-13 Diesel offers the classic marijuana experience: a peaceful smile, a relaxed body, and a renewed appreciation for tasty snacks. This is a smoke for sunny days and happy times with friends. Rather than a trip to the shopping mall or other frenzied environments, enjoy it on a slow afternoon in a cozy spot at home or in the great outdoors.

Variety Stability
Ed Rosenthal

"Stable" and "unstable" are often used to describe characteristics of varieties. When I've asked marijuana growers what this means, they usually discuss plants that, like chameleons, change with time, location, or some other environmental condition.

The definition that breeders use for stability has to do with the variety, rather than the plant. Imagine a field of crops that grow in uniform rows, such as corn. Each of these plants, which were grown from seed, looks almost identical to the rest. What do we know about it? The plants could be a stable variety or an F1 hybrid. Stable varieties have a homogeneous gene pool, they are very close genetically. A true F1 hybrid plant is a cross between two stable varieties. All the new plants have received similar genetics. As a result, the plants are almost identical.

Landraces

In nature, landraces—that is, plant populations that have grown in a specific physical environment for many generations—are usually homogeneous in tropical areas. The reason is that these regions typically have consistent weather from year to year. The varieties that fall into this category are equatorial sativas and their progeny including Hazes, Brazilians, Colombians, Central Africans and other landraces that grow between the equator and 20 degree latitude.

In temperate and mild climates, the weather is more variable—one year it's rainy, the next sunny. Plant populations are more heterogeneous in these regions because this increases their ability to deal with variable weather. Depending on the conditions, some plants will thrive while others are more stressed. Because the weather differs from one year to the next, the heterogeneity allows some plants from the same

One variety of Oregon creeper. Here the main stem stops growing but new branches grow below. They creep.

Although mostly sativa, Super Silver Haze has an unusual asymmetry which may be due in part to the heavy foliage and flowers on the branches.

gene pool to do well while others struggle. Which plants thrive and which plants experience stress depends on their compatibility with that year's weather patterns. How can these plants adapt to varying conditions, in contrast to their homogenous cousins? Heterogeneity is a result of having different alleles, different versions of genes. Since the plants are pollinating each other, even alleles that are not bene-

ficial in a given year are carried forward. Landraces that originate in temperate areas are found between the 25th and 30th parallels. They include Afghanis, Indicas, and Lebanese, Moroccan and Mexican strains. Only when the weather pattern remains consistent for three or four years will it become apparent that the plants are becoming more homogeneous.

Alien Trainwrek: This purple beauty grows in bush form. It sends hundreds of medium sized spikes into the air, pincushion style.

True Breeding Strains

All modern marijuana strains are progeny of landraces. For instance, Skunk #1 is a combination of Oaxacan, Colombian Gold (probably Santa Marta Gold) and Afghani. The Skunk #1 breeder developed the F1 hybrid, and then followed this artistry with more by making Skunk #1 into a true breeding strain. Creating a true breeding strain requires a keen eye, nose and head in selecting parents for the subsequent crosses.

The theory is that by selecting from a smaller and smaller population of plants with similar characteristics, the variation in alleles between plants will even-tually become very small, resulting in a true breeding strain. Techniques used to achieve this include inbreeding, that is, breeding sibling plants; backcrossing, which is crossing a plant with one of a previous generation; and self crossing, or crossing a plant to itself using induced hermaphroditism.

What does all of this mean to the home gardener contemplating buying a packet of seeds? A true breeding strain can be very useful to people who plant seed to harvest bud. Conventional farmers use true growing seeds for the same reason. All the plants have the same characteristics and are ready at the same time. These strains are appropriate for the grower who wants a consistent and uniform crop.

The Advantages of Unstable Strains

Gardeners who buy seeds to choose clone mothers have a different set of goals. They have additional concerns beyond the yield they will get from the first or trial garden of seeds. These gardeners are involved in a selection process. They're looking for one exceptional plant that stands out from the rest in some way to carry their garden forward. When this is a part of the gardener's goals, s/he is better off using F2 hybrids or unstable varieties. Plants grown from unstable seeds will exhibit some variation, which allows the grower to select the best one for his cannabis preferences and gardening goals.

An unnamed local varietiy adapted to inland Oregon grows straight spikes at a 45 degree angle from the main stem.

There are several different kinds of unstable varieties: F2 Hybrids, Partially Inbred, Four-Way Crosses, and Hidden Recessive.

F2 Hybrids

When two stable varieties (P1) are crossed, the first generation hybrid (F1) is uniform. Not so when the F1 generation is crossed to itself. Each F1 plant contains a combination of genes from each parent, with random combinations of alleles. When F1s are crossed amongst themselves, these random combinations may allow the plants to exhibit qualities that would otherwise be recessive. F2 plants usually exhibit various combinations of the original two P1 parents. This may provide the grower with a lot of choices regarding growth habits and psychoactive qualities.

Partially Inbred

It requires six or seven generations of inbreeding to develop a variety that breeds true when it is crossed to itself. It also requires skill and talent, as well as clear goals. When the goals deviate, previous work may be rendered obsolete. Without skill at selecting crosses, the goals can never be reached. Even more pressing, when the market calls, breeders often offer varieties that haven't been completely refined. While this is not desirable for gardeners planning to grow a crop from seeds, it offers the gardener who is choosing clone mothers many opportunities.

Romulan Variety: An indica/sativa hybrid has lost its symmetry and grew long thick branches in all directions Eventually these branches had to be staked because they were so heavy with buds.

Four-Way Crosses

Sometimes breeders cross two pairs of inbred lines to make two different F1 hybrids. Then the F1 hybrids are crossed together. Because there are so many combinations of alleles possible, and because the genes are so mixed up, it may take eight to ten generations to achieve a true breeding variety. Usually breeders release the new cross after five or six inbreeding crosses and then continue to refine the cross as they are selling seeds. As a result the Four-Way you bought a few years ago may look somewhat different than the one you buy this year.

Hidden Recessives

Once in a while a variety will be offered that comes in two versions or phenotypes. The notes will state that most of the plants will have a particular characteristic, but a small minority of the plants, usually one-quarter, one-sixth, or one-eighth of them, exhibit a different characteristic. It could be something as inconsequential as leaf size, but sometimes the two versions of the plants are dramatically different. What's happening here is that the minority version carries recessive alleles of a single or several genes. They are expressed only when there is no dominant

Ruderalis F1 hybrid with a sativa was grown outdoors. It started flowering at the third set of leaves, but the flowers never ripened into big buds. The effect was almost a headache rather than a high.

allele in the pair. For example, two F1 hybrids have both a dominant allele (A) and a recessive (a). When they are crossed, the statistical outcome is one AA plant, two Aa plants, and one aa plant. In the three plants with an A in the mix (the AA and the two Aa's), the dominant characteristic will be present. Only the aa will exhibit the recessive characteristic. When recessive characteristics show up, it's an indication that the strain has not been "cleaned" of the recessive genes.

Gardeners have lots of choices. Not only are there hundreds of varieties, but they come either as F1 hybrids and true breeding strains, which produce nearly identical plants, or as F2 and only partially inbred varieties, which produce a range of similar plants. No matter what gardening goals you may have, there are a bounty of good selections available.

One of Nevil's flowering rooms at the Seed Bank. Many plants were trialed in this space. Dutch regulations now forbid this work.

A legal field in Khandwa, India circa 1981. The plants were a single sativa variety and were quite uniform. This landrace is now grown only furtively. Brown plants were suffering from *Frusairum wilt*, which was indigenous to the fields.

Gonzo #1

Reservoir Seeds

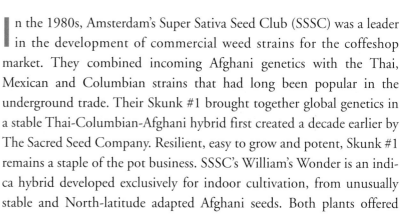

 IS 85I/15S

 narcotic

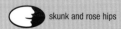 skunk and rose hips

 60-70 days

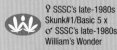 ♀ SSSC's late-1980s Skunk#1/Basic 5 x ♂ SSSC's late-1980s William's Wonder

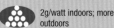 2g/watt indoors; more outdoors

 SOG

In the 1980s, Amsterdam's Super Sativa Seed Club (SSSC) was a leader in the development of commercial weed strains for the coffeshop market. They combined incoming Afghani genetics with the Thai, Mexican and Columbian strains that had long been popular in the underground trade. Their Skunk #1 brought together global genetics in a stable Thai-Columbian-Afghani hybrid first created a decade earlier by The Sacred Seed Company. Resilient, easy to grow and potent, Skunk #1 remains a staple of the pot business. SSSC's William's Wonder is an indica hybrid developed exclusively for indoor cultivation, from unusually stable and North-latitude adapted Afghani seeds. Both plants offered growers a fast and consistent harvest, and gave coffeeshop patrons a strong narcotic stone with a bit of sativa uplift. It is to these ganja classics that Reservoir turned when customers begged for "a fat skunky indica that'd rip your head off." The result is Gonzo #1. Reservoir reccomends smoking Gonzo #1 while listening to Pink Floyd's *The Dark Side of the Moon* or having Tantric sex.

Gonzo #1 plants show some phenotypic variation. Some plants have a skunky pungency, while others smell sweeter, like a rose bush, and offer a slightly more euphoric high. All Gonzo #1 plants develop in a classic profile, suitable for either multi-branch or SOG cultivation. They have thick, indica-type leaves, and are very mite-resistant.

Gonzo #1 finishes growth at a compact 4 feet (130 cm) and flowers over $8^1/_2$ to 10 weeks. Indoor growers can easily achieve yields of 2 grams per watt; outdoor yields can be much higher.

What is "gonzo?" The word was popularized by counterculture hero Dr. Hunter S. Thompson, in whose memory Reservoir named this strain. It's been said to derive from an Italian-American slang term meaning "crazy," or a French-Canadian word for a pathway that shines in a dark forest. Those are probably lies; if there was ever an exact definition, Dr. Thompson took it with him to his grave. "Gonzo" is a word the devil whispered in Hunter Thompson's ear on one of the good doctor's epic binges. Gonzo #1 is a strain for the wild at heart, a liberating, euphoric accompaniment when seeking adventure.

Grandaddy Grape Ape

Apothecary

positive, alert

grape

60 days/Oct. 15

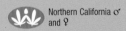
Northern California ♂ and ♀

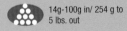
14g-100g in/ 254 g to 5 lbs. out

Apothecary specializes in creating medical strains. They have been growing and refining this all-indica variety for five years. Her ancestors have grown in the hills of Northern California for over two decades, where her phenotypes have been known by many different names including Grape Ape, Purple Erkel and Granddaddy Purple.

As an indoor crop, Grandaddy Grape Ape is equally happy in hydro or soil. With a pure indica heritage, this plant is predisposed to a short bushy stature. Grandaddy branches extensively, making her less than ideal for SOG style grows, but she can be trained to make an awesome super crop garden. When left to her natural tendencies, this strain will make a nice big shrub that reaches about 3 feet (1 m) indoors or up to 8 feet (2.6 m) outdoors. She is a hardy grower with tight internodes and dense dark green to purple leaves.

Grandaddy Grape Ape is easy to work with throughout her growth cycle. She likes a cool temperature, between 70-80°F (23-26°C), and can be very forgiving so long as she is adequately watered. Due to her high resin output and dense structure, this plant can be alluring to mites.

Grandaddy Grape Ape finishes her flowering cycle in 8-9 weeks. The buds are dense green nuggets that gain royal purple hues as they mature. Depending on the size she is allowed to reach, Grandaddy Grape Ape can yield between $^1/_2$ ounce (14 g) to 3.5 ounces (100 g) apiece. Outdoor plants will really deliver, with potential yields between 8 ounces and 5 pounds (0.25 – 2.5 kg).

There is a potent, undeniable grape tinge to this plant's aroma, and a sweet grape taste that lingers subtly on the tongue. Grandaddy Grape Ape's effects are enduring, with a smooth even feeling throughout. For an indica, her buzz is surprisingly alert and energetic rather than sedating. This is a good smoke for walking in the high meadows and swimming in the lake afterwards. Medicinally, this variety has given relief to cancer/chemotherapy patients. Grandaddy Grape Ape has taken first prize in no less than four pot competitions: The Inglewood Medical Cannabis Cup in 2004, and the Green Cup in 2004, 2005 and 2006.

Grape Krush

DJ Short

Right photo: Ed Rosenthal

 60I/40S

 sedate, social, creeper

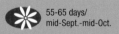 musky, sweet

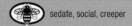 55-65 days/ mid-Sept.-mid-Oct.

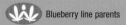 Blueberry line parents

 25-50 g/ft.²

Grape Krush belongs to the Blueberry family bred by DJ Short. The Blueberry strains mix indica with haze for a combination of happy stone and easy, adaptable cultivation. Specifically, the indica genes give the plants a shorter growing season than the slow-growing and sometimes finicky hazes. Blueberries tend toward a blue tint in the leaves and a berry flavor in the smoke. Within the Blueberry family, Grape Krush is the peaceful child. This strain's high is physically soothing, but still haze-y enough to keep a conversation flowing.

Grape Krush was developed for indoor growing, but can flourish outdoors as well—even as far north as Holland—especially if given organic nutrients. Indoors, she prefers soil but adapts well to hydroponic systems, too. In general, DJ Short recommends light feeding with nitrogen and organic nutrients; however, Grape Krush loves all of the good worm castings and bat guano she can get.

Grape Krush branches bushy, especially when topped. Like her Blueberry relatives, she is dark green to purple with lavender/red hues. She has thicker and more variegated leaves than the other Blueberries. The larger calyxes on her bulkier, more "rounded" buds show a distinctive fox-tailing structure late in her flowering cycle. Her variegated leaves sometimes curl or "krinkle;" this is an expression of anomalous recessed traits from her diverse ancestors, not a mutation that indicates an unhealthy plant.

Grape Krush finishes in approximately 8-9 weeks indoors, or from late September to mid-late October outdoors. She is medium in height and heavy in yield—25 to 50 grams (1-2 oz.) per square foot at 50 watts per square foot, or up to 1 gram per watt under optimal conditions.

Growing plants have a strong odor, both sweet and musky. The harvest from this strain is connoisseur-grade bud with a sweetish smoke. The high comes on very slowly, building up for as much as an hour, and then settles in for the night – a bit more like a pot brownie stone than the usual smoker's rush. Traces of haze in the stone add inspiration to the conversation, and some radiant dreams or fantasies at bedtime. It's a relaxing and social effect, like red wine, and a good antidote to social anxiety.

Hashberry

Mandala Seeds

Hashberry is the unique result of a rigorous selection from desirable parents, one of which contains landrace genetics from Kashmir, North India—home to generations of great hashish. This mostly indica strain is suitable for indoor and outdoor climates, performing best out in nature in the latitudes between 45 degrees North and South, and in climates that have a dry autumn season. Indoors, this variety does well in all grow systems, including sea of green.

Mandala has paid special attention to the preservation of this hybrid's vigor. Outdoors, Hashberry is a hardy strain with a thick stem structure to carry her heavy load of buds. Her average flowering time is $8^1/_2$ to $9^1/_2$ weeks. Outdoor plants in warmer climates will finish at the end of September, while temperate areas require an additional few weeks. Flowering times outdoors can be shortened by as much as two weeks if well established clones are transplanted around summer solstice. In organic indoor grows, you can almost do without feeding; an adequate pot size and quality potting soil is all you need for optimal results.

Mandala recommends allowing seedlings to reach 8-10 inches (20-25 cm) and then forcing flowering. Using this method, growers can expect an average yield of 450-500 grams (16-18 oz.) per square meter under 400 watts per square meter. This is an easy plant to grow and shows good heat resistance. Its medium-sized stature makes Hashberry a good selection when space is at a premium. There are two distinct phenotypes: one is shorter and develops branches that reach up to the middle of the plant; the other is slightly taller with almost no branching. Both are perfect for close planting, but the branchy type should be given a bit of extra space for better light dispersal.

Hashberry carries an extremely heavy main cola that dominates the plant structure and contributes to her above-average yields. The cola offers a delicious aroma, and an old school high and taste. Many old-timers have reported that smoking this strain reminds them of the finest Columbian grass of the 1970s, an effect Mandala refers to as "vintage

 mostly indica

 relaxing, head/body balance

 blackcurrent jam, hashy

 60-65 days

 ♀ indica from California x ♂ strain with land race genetics from Kashmir, North India

 450-500 g/m²

 below 45˚N latitude

 SOG

deja-vú." This strain is easy to trim and the dried buds have great "bag appeal."

Young flowering plants develop a fruity-floral aroma that smells like blueberry or blackcurrent jam. Some plants have a more spicy note mixed in with the fruity-floral bouquet. As flowering and resin production progresses, a hashy aroma also sets in. Other plants have a minty-peppery taste to them that is equally pleasant.

As the name suggests, Hashberry is a great variety for the hashish fan. The high starts out very clear and builds slowly into a classic chill-out vibe with a relaxing and balanced head-body effect. Toward the end, a more body-oriented phase sets in that nevertheless leaves you able to be social and active. Hashberry is perfect when used to relax and unwind in the evening, or to alleviate stress and pain.

Hash Heaven

Soma Seeds

Right photo: Ed Rosenthal

 50S/50I

 up, creeper

 hashy, tangy

 70-84 days

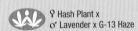 ♀ Hash Plant x ♂ Lavender x G-13 Haze

 40-60 g/plant

Hash Heaven is one of several crosses Soma has made from the G-13 genetics brought to Amsterdam by the seed breeder Neville in the 1980s. Neville successfully crossed G-13 (an indica strain developed in the Northwest) with classic haze genetics to produce a strong, kind and balanced stone. Soma acquired the G-13 Haze from Neville and carefully added its sweet strength to the signature qualities of several other varieties. Here, strains have been crossed with an eye toward hash production and quality, for growers who put hash first. If you put hash first, this strain promises a little piece of Hash Heaven.

This 50/50 hybrid is a hardy plant that pulls through adversities, but getting this plant to perform at its optimum requires a little previous growing experience on the resume. Hash Heaven is suitable for indoor grows unless you are in a semi-tropical location with a long growing season. Soma recommends potting in soil with bat guano and other organic nutrients.

Hash Heaven branches extensively and delivers an impressive per plant yield of 40-60 grams, while staying at a manageable size of 4-5 feet (130-160cm). This is Soma's highest-yielding plant, a reward for the grower's patience during the 10-12 week flowering cycle before harvesting.

Her colas are dark green bananas of impressively firm, compact flowers framed by minimal foliage. The dank and spicy hash smell starts to emanate from these plants shortly after they enter the flowering phase, and delivers in the final product as a satisfying hashy tang.

Hash Heaven has been lovingly bred by a devotee to hash, Soma himself. This strain offers a functional and awake high—a sweet cream poured in the coffee of your day, preferably a day of active play rather than intense work. The buzz is a creeper that takes its time landing, but once it does it can carry you through an afternoon in a pleasantly invigorated yet laid back state. Soma recommends this variety as a compliment to a little afternoon delight with your sweetheart. Medical marijuana users have found it to be a strong antidote for many types of chronic pain.

Soma's garden

Haze Mist

Flying Dutchmen

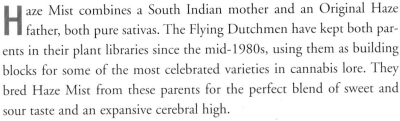

S

euphoric, busy, heady

spicy, sweet-sour

95-100 days/end Nov.

♀ South Indian (P1) x
♂ Skunk no. 1 (P1)

200-300 g/m²

below 30° N latitudes
greenhouse

SOG

aze Mist combines a South Indian mother and an Original Haze father, both pure sativas. The Flying Dutchmen have kept both parents in their plant libraries since the mid-1980s, using them as building blocks for some of the most celebrated varieties in cannabis lore. They bred Haze Mist from these parents for the perfect blend of sweet and sour taste and an expansive cerebral high.

Haze Mist is a pure sativa, very tall and slender with lime green leaves and long internode spaces. She can be grown indoors, in a greenhouse, or outdoors at latitudes below 30 degrees North. Outdoor-grown Haze Mist reaches up to 13 feet (4 m) tall and has consistently survived Dutch winters. The natural home for these plants, however, is in tropical or semi-tropical locales where photoperiod fluctuations are minor and growing seasons are lengthier. In the tropics, she matures in 14-16 weeks from seed (12-14 weeks from cutting) and yields 10-17 ounces (300-500 g).

Indoors, Haze Mist can easily be cultivated with a little knowledge of pure sativa types. The best results come from growing her in rich, well-drained soil, high in organic matter. The Dutchmen usually grow their seedlings under 14 hours of light, then take cuttings from each seedling, and root them at 10 hours of light, until they show sex. Cuttings from female seedlings are then transplanted and flowered at 12 hours of light. If they have not matured at 12 weeks of flowering, the breeders reduce the light photoperiod by 30 minutes per week until the cuttings have matured.

Haze Mist enjoys a medium-strength nutrient regime, slowly increased throughout the cycle, then flushing at the end. High nitrogen levels have a detrimental effect, which is indicated if leaves lose their healthy lime green color. These plants can be pruned back until the fourth week of flowering; alternatively, they can be pruned back once or twice early on, and then later tied or staked down. They will continue to grow for around 8 weeks under a 12/12 photocycle. Indoor yields vary greatly depending on the style of

growing. On average, Haze Mist produces 200-250 grams (7-9 oz.) per square meter, but with a little more headroom, 4-6 plants per square meter could harvest substantially more.

As the plants mature, they form long slender buds with a spicy sweet scent. The round bracts swell to bursting around harvest time, as the buds shift from lime green to gold with occasional purple tints. The end product smells and tastes very spicy with subtle, sweet undertones. Haze Mist's high is soaring and energetic with no "body." This is one of the few strains that has no ceiling: once you go beyond high, the effect becomes psychedelic. Prolonged heavy use is not recommended: too much pure haze makes many people twitchy and nervous. In moderation, however, the high is perfect for all active pursuits, and lends itself well to artistic and musical endeavors.

Ice Cream

Paradise Seeds

Photos: Trichome Pharm

Paradise Seeds' Ice Cream expresses a diversity of phenotypes, all of them producing good, tasty smoke. The plants look extremely uniform when started from seeds until the fourth week of bloom, when bud formation and final stretching creates some differences in flower formation and node pattern. The common theme among all phenotypes is extreme rapid growth and vitality, with healthy large dark green leaves and profuse resin production. Another common theme is a smooth, creamy taste that reminded Paradise of ice cream.

Some phenotypes express a "sativa" growth pattern, with extremely thin serrated leaves, a high calyx-to-leaf ratio and a slightly hallucinogenic high. All Ice Cream plants give out copious amounts of trichomes, sometimes exhibiting an extremely tight formation of army-style rows of large resin heads. Paradise bred this especially productive phenotype for its almost geometric resin pattern. It delivered some generous hashish extraction, yielding an average of 45 grams per 1000 watts of light input of premium quality ice extraction bubble hash in two extractions. Ice Cream hashish has already become popular with Montreal aficionados.

Ice Cream is a very fast grower, finishing in 55-60 days indoors in hydro or soil, or by early October outdoors. She almost doubles in size when put into flowering after one month of vegetative growth, becoming a middle-sized plant when she finishes. Ice Cream is good as a sea of green or a multi-branch plant. Her stems and branches are very flexible and offer a great opportunity to take advantage of tying down and bending techniques.

This strain's metabolism runs extremely "hi-revolutions" and responds well to multiple horticultural triggers. Call it a sports car of growth. "It's all good and beautiful to own a Ferrari," cautions the breeder, "but you have to know how to drive it." Ice Cream's fast response tendencies, especially in hydroponics, make her sensitive to adverse conditions. Her part-sativa heritage makes her somewhat tolerant to heat and humidity, but she

 60I/40S

 trippy, equal head and body

 creamy vanilla with undertones of skunk and pine

 55-60 days/early Oct.

 mostly sativa resinous ♀ x reversed female sweet stout indica ♀

 500 g/m² in/out

 between 50° N and S latitude

 SOG

will show other stresses (cold, overfeeding) very clearly. She is especially sensitive to moisture level fluctuations at the root zone. Use caution with feeding, and pay attention to light distance from the plants.

Ice Cream cultivators find themselves engulfed in sweet smells as they train the plant's profuse lateral branching and promote her fat main cola. The slightest touch sends up a perfume of plant sugars. The buds themselves are white and frosty, with a hint of vanilla. The smoke is smooth, with faint undertones of skunk and pine.

Just as Ice Cream's metabolism roars along with multiple cycles and variations, likewise her stone is a series of revolutions, an antidote to stoner boredom. Her effects are well balanced and register on both head and body levels, but in stages, alternating from cerebral to slightly physical in a back and forth motion within the same smoking session. For both gardeners and tokers, Ice Cream offers vigor and diversity under a smooth vanilla coating.

Jack the Ripper

TGA Seeds

Photos: Subcool

Jack The Ripper is a product of TGA breeder Subcool's experiments in using outcrosses to boost the quality of backcrossed strains—in this case, blending a Space Queen male into a cubed backcrossing to work toward the original, F1 strain of Jacks Cleaner.

"The cool part is the outcrosses are sometimes better than the parent strains," says Subcool. "I feel this is the case with Jack the Ripper. The lemon tart of Jacks Cleaner has combined with the candy mango flavor of the Space Queen to create a resinous marvel." This cross is notable for its intense lemon smell, which while strong enough to discourage insects, does not really suggest pot—meaning that Jack the Ripper, like her fearsome namesake, might permanently evade the noses of the law.

Jack the Ripper's seeds are huge, and may require help shucking their hull. Once plants are started, they are hardy and easy to clone, making them suitable for first-time growers. Trifoliate seedlings, and two plants from one seed, are both common occurences. Jack the Ripper grows well outdoors in warm climates, or indoors in large bushes or SOG-style. When these plants are given moderate feeding and allowed to bush out, they finish in 8-9 weeks as a frost-covered miniature Christmas tree, just over 3 feet (1 m) tall. They may need an extra week or two of vegetative growth to compete with taller strains in a canopy.

JTR is a compact plant with dark, serrated leaves and tight colas attached to a study trunk. The plant's five to seven leaves can show pink veining if exposed to cool air, and may curl up around the third week of budding, like the leaves of a venus flytrap, as they become plastered with heavy resin. Indeed, growers will see very little green on this plant by harvest time; instead, she will be covered by an icy mantle of trichomes, like a dwarf spruce buried by winter. This promises a good yield of bubble hash or dry kief. Bud yields average 3-4 ounces (90-120 grams) per plant.

Jack the Ripper hits you behind the eyes with an almost lemon-cleaner palate and a jolt-

 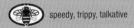 80S/20I

 speedy, trippy, talkative

 lemon

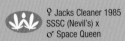 56-63 days

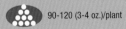 ♀ Jacks Cleaner 1985 SSSC (Nevil's) x ♂ Space Queen

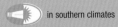 90-120 (3-4 oz.)/plant

 in southern climates

SOG

ing sativa buzz. About five minutes after this first rush, a long elation settles on the smoker, sometimes followed by munchies and drowsiness after a few hours. Anecdotally, medicinal users have reported an analgesic, almost body-numbing effect. Jack the Ripper has gotten many thank-yous for alleviating chronic pains. The mental side of the high leans toward happiness, chattiness, and trippy visual distortions, with potential for paranoia when indulged in heavily. Subcool notes that the lemon taste gets sweeter the longer these buds are cured.

The Story of Jack the Ripper
Subcool

The story Jack the Ripper is a fine example of what can happen along the way during a breeding project. I have always wanted to have Jacks Cleaner in seed form. People suggested that I self her but I don't believe in that type of breeding. I feel a male plays a vital role in breeding projects.

About six years ago I outcrossed Jacks Cleaner with Blueberry. Two years ago I backcrossed this Jacks Cleaner x Blueberry with Jacks Cleaner and created Jacks Cleaner backcross. Even though the JC backcross kicks ass, has won awards and is used in breeding projects, it was not what I was looking for. Around that time I grew out BCGA's Space Queen bred by Vic High and found it to be some of the best weed I ever smoked. When working with fellow TGA breeder MzJill, we found an amazing Space Queen male. MzJill used it in crosses that resulted in the Jillybean and Spacejill strains. We started calling him "Space Dude," and after some deliberation, we decided that he was a much better candidate for outcrossing with Jacks Cleaner. So we passed the Jacks Cleaner backcross and Jacks Cleaner Blueberry to other members of TGA and started over.

Using our standard breeding methods we worked with Jacks Cleaner and Space Dude, and started a test run of new seeds. This new hybrid had one weird trait—twin seedlings. We started seeds using rapid rooters with no pre-soaking. I never pamper test runs. Once seedlings sprouted and developed nice roots I transplanted them into 1-gallon containers and placed them under a 400-watt light. When the plants matured, the males were taken to a separate area, the best females were tagged and the rest were tossed. We ended up with three females that met our selection criteria. Collectively, this cross became Jack the Ripper.

In test runs, I feed only with water during the entire cycle to test the plant's natural ability to produce without being pushed. These three females were topped, trained and vegged for about 45 days. They reached a size of 24 inches with multiple growing heads. Once in flowering, the plants quickly started swelling with buds and by day 25, copious amounts of resin had become visible. At week 3, the plants had the first hints of the lemon fragrance that I was looking for. One female stretched so much that I had to bend her severely to keep her approximately equal with the others. I am happy to report that all three plants had the exact mango lemon smell I was seeking.

In addition to other qualities, a breeding goal was to shorten the grow time, and at 50 days, we were on track. With the exception of the one tall lady, all three JTR females were very similar. To avoid numerical confusion we gave each JTR female a distinct name. Lemango became the tall one that looked more Space Queen dominant. Soylent Green had the largest colas, and the plant most resembling Jacks Cleaner with her predictable resin leaf curl was given the name Pink Lemonade. This final plant is the one that became the star during multiple sessions in front of my lens.

I feel Jack the Ripper represents the sum of what I've learned and collected as a breeder. To succeed in creating crosses that maintain the exact desirable traits of the mother that I wanted while improving other specific qualities is a humbling experience.

Jacky White ♀♀

Paradise Seeds

 75S/25I

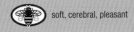 soft, cerebral, pleasant

 grapefruit

 60 days/mid-Oct.

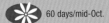 mostly sativa

 600 grams/m² in; 600/plant out

L ike Jackie Brown, the working-class heroine created by Pam Grier and Quentin Tarantino, Jacky White is tough, fine looking, mellow, and pure woman—that is, her seeds are 100% female, an attractive feature for first-time growers who can be intimidated by the task of sexing the plants. Beginners will also appreciate Jacky's hardiness, high yield, fast finish, and striking profile; this is a truly aesthetically beautiful plant. This mostly sativa hybrid is also notable for her stability, with only slight variations between individual plants.

Outdoors, Jacky White likes a moderate to sunny climate. Indoors, hydro, coco, and soil are all excellent growing mediums. She likes to branch, so the garden setup that optimizes yield on these plants would allow a bit more space for the side branches to fully develop. Pruning or bending to increase yield works well with this strain.

Jacky White smells like a grapefruit tree all through her flowering period, which finishes in 60 days at most, with an abundance of chunky colas glittering and luminescent with resin. Her indoor harvest is impressive—1 gram per watt of light per square meter, or up to 600g per square meter under a 600-watt high-pressure sodium light. Outside harvests are predictably larger.

Jacky White's growing style is sativa-like, with a note of good indica qualities (ease, hardiness, fast finish); likewise, her stone is sativa-like with a hint of indica to take off sativa's speedy edge. She offers a clear, mind-lofting cerebral high accompanied by a pleasant body buzz. Her stone has a smooth entry and exit that many will find inviting, with an enduring effect, although the rich haze-citrus taste may have tokers reloading their bongs anyway. Since she came on the scene in 2005, Jacky White has proven popular with German and Austrian connoisseurs. Like her cinema namesake, this attractive lady is likely to warrant attention that will move her into the big time.

Paradise's Feminised Seeds

Clones are a good alternative to feminised seeds. The production of feminised seed is not that easy, and has some pitfalls. Some of the feminised seeds available commercially partly turn hermaphrodite. The reason is that candidate plants are not carefully selected. Paradise Seeds uses only female plants that do not turn hermaphrodite even under stress. Then we treat this plant to induce the growth of stamins, which produce pollen. This pollen is then used to fertilize appropriate sister plants. This method is called "selfing," that is, crossing a plant to itself.

The seeds produced using this method will grow uniform superior female plants with abundant flowers. We believe that plants from seeds are much better than clones since they are stronger and more resilient.

Jilly Bean

TGA Seeds

Jilly Bean is the first strain bred by Green Avengers member MzJill. Her friend Charmed, another female grower, suggested the name. Like jelly beans, Jilly "Beans" are seeds that promise a sweet, fruit-flavored, happy-making treat.

Jilly Bean is easy to grow both indoors and out. When grown outside, this strain does best in dry, warm climates, where frost or rains don't occur until after mid-September. One fan of Jilly Bean has grown very successfully in Israel, using outdoor soil alone and no nutrients. Indoors, Jilly Bean adapts to either soil or hydro, and can be grown as a single-cola plant in SOG. She yields best as a large bush, topped several times, giving many large dense colas.

Jilly Bean has a light to average nutrient requirement. This strain is adaptable to higher grow room temperatures, but for maximum yields, the temperature should stay below 85°F when the lights are on. Jilly Bean will purple up if the dark time temperature is allowed to drop by 20 degrees or more, producing reddish or burgundy velvet leaves inherited from her Orange Velvet mother. Her leaves become darker and more leathery as she matures. The cooler the nighttime temperature, the more magnificent the hues of this lady will become.

Jilly Bean seeds express two phenotypes. One stays short and bushy with a lot of lateral branching. The other grows taller, with little lateral branching. When Jilly Bean is flowered between 24 and 32 inches in height, she finishes at approximately 4 feet (120 cm).

Jilly Bean buds grow in a pointy shape. They are dense and rock-hard from top to bottom, and forest-green in color, with some red hairs, and plenty of sticky resin. In good light and organic soil, this plant yields 3-4 ounces of primo sticky nugs. With an extra week of vegetative time, she can become even more robust. Grown in a hydroponic bubbler system, this plant can yield 10 or more ounces. It wafts the odor of sweet overripe

 70I/30S

 creeper, mind/body relaxation

 mango candy

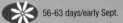 56-63 days/early Sept.

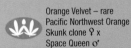 Orange Velvet – rare Pacific Northwest Orange Skunk clone ♀ x Space Queen ♂

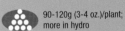 90-120g (3-4 oz.)/plant; more in hydro

 SOG

mangos, pineapples, and oranges with a candied over-tone. The pungency means it can be smelled from over a yard away, but doesn't have the classic "marijuana smell."

Her palate, too, is like pulpy citrus and candy, which makes her a tasty (as well as toasty) ingredient for cannabis bakers. Smokers will also enjoy the jellybean taste for its own sake. Her stone warms up slowly, speading evenly over mind and body. Mellow, giddy, and friendly, this is a good daytime smoke, and one that has been reported to alleviate chronic pain and depression.

Kaya

Nirvana Seed Bank

Nirvana created this strain as a mellow sativa option for novice indoor growers, and outdoor growers in rough climates. They started with a beautiful, hardy, stable Mexican sativa, reminiscent of old strains in her more mellow potency and agreable nature. This strain was crossed with Top 44, one of their best selling commercial varieties. Top 44 has become popular in Holland for her easy cultivation, fast finish (just over six weeks in perfect conditions), and compact profile. Nirvana breeders forced a female Top 44 to develop male flowers using giberellic acid. The resulting strain, Kaya, is feminized, meaning that all her seeds are females. These parents have produced an easygoing plant that beginners will enjoy growing.

Kaya finishes in 8-9 weeks indoors, or around October 1 outdoors in Spain or similar climates. She is resistant to pests and tolerates heat well. When grown indoors, her compact branching makes her a good candidate for sea of green. Her branches grow outward in moderation and stay thick enough to hold her buds, so when grown as a multi-branch plant, pruning and branch supports are seldom necessary. Outdoors, or in a greenhouse with huge pots of soil, Kaya can also be grown to huge sizes. She performs best when allowed to reach around a meter before inducing flowering. The plants will finish around 6 feet (2 m). Because of her hardiness, Kaya is a good plant for outdoor guerilla grows, perfect for leaving somewhere with a global positioning system and finding again in the autumn.

Kaya has a spicy flavor, refreshingly different from skunk, with a sweet kiss that lingers on the tongue. The high is also different from the punchout associated with some popular "skunk" strains—a return to the mellower potencies of days gone by. "Lighter highs," says Nirvana, "definitely have their place and their fans." Kaya is unlikely to waylay lightweight smokers on the first bong hit, and she is a great daytime friend to those who prefer a high that is more like a "snack" than a "meal," a stone that is easier to moderate. For both gardeners and tokers, Kaya is easy to get along with.

 55I/45S

 mild, refreshing

 spicy, sweet

 56-63 days/Oct.

 Mexican sativa x Top 44

 350-450 dried g/m² in SOG

 greenhouse

 SOG

The Secret Chemistry of Cannabis Odors and Highs

Ed Rosenthal

Books like the *Big Book of Buds* series are possible because of the diversity in marijuana varieties. Think of how different cannabis would be if this were not the case! The terrific subtleties of this plant allow gardeners with different goals to strive for their ideal plant, and marijuana enthusiasts to explore the different effects and odors that this plant has to offer.

We have often heard that varieties of marijuana taste different and create different highs because they contain different ratios of cannabinoids, the chemicals specific to marijuana. However, when modern marijuana was tested for cannabinoids, there was a big spike at delta-9 THC, but all the other cannabinoids, including cannabinol (CBN), cannabdiol (CBD), cannabichromene (CBC) and cannabigerol (CBG) were scarcely noted. In 2005, scientists testing CBD, which was considered the main modifier of THC's effects, noticed that it didn't dock at the CB1 receptor site in the brain—where THC locks in and sets off the chemical cascade that results in altered awareness. They did find, however, that CBD has many medicinal qualities even though it is not psychoactive.

If cannabinoids other than THC are not causing the high then we must look at other ingredients in the smoke-stream. Terpenes are major components of marijuana resin. These molecules make up the largest percentage of the content of essential oils contained in many plants. Most of them have a boiling point above water, but still readily evaporate in the air. The scents of most flowers, herbs and spices are composed of these oils.

Chemically speaking, terpenes are composed of repeating units of isoprene, which is a five-carbon unit chain or ring with eight hydrogen atoms attached(C5H8). Terpenes use the simple isoprene unit as blocks to build 10, 15, 20 and 30 carbon units* and can twist and turn the molecular structure

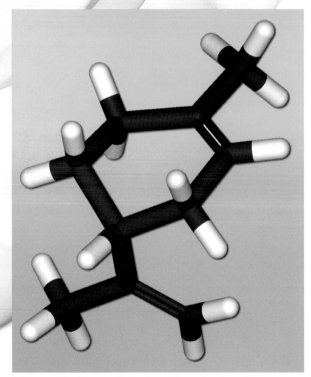

D-Limonene, the terpene with the classic citrus odor. The carbon atoms are black, the attached hydrogen molecules are white (C10, H16).

* These are called, respectively, the C10-monoterpenoid, C15-sesquiterpenoid, C20-diterpenoid, C-30 triterpenoid.

Since plants are not mobile, they can't outrun predators or pick up and relocate when competing plants move into the neighborhood. As a result, they have amassed other defenses against predators and competitors. One of their main strategies is chemical warfare. We use essential oils which are concentrates of compounds designed by plants for various tasks. Some repel enemies, others kill, sicken, delay maturation or affect the metabolism of predators. Plants use other aromatics to attract pollinators for reproduction or to attract enemies' predators.

to form simple chains or three-dimensional (polycyclic) structures. In addition, terpenes can form bonds with other molecules, which affect how animals and plants react to them. Depending on how they stack against each other, they form different aromatic compounds.

Most of the aromas that we associate with plants are the result of terpenes and flavonoids. Humans can smell and taste these compounds, but that is not the only ways that they affect us. Aromatherapy uses inhaled essential oils to regulate mood, sleep patterns, acuity, and healing processes. Lavender oil is a soothing agent and relaxant; rosemary is used to focus attention and provide a sense of satisfaction. These effects are a result of the combination of terpenes and other chemicals found in the oils of these plants. While terpenes affect the brain in their own way, they also modify the effect of THC within the brain, adding subtleties to the high.

Some terpenes may affect the high in this way because they lock into receptor sites in the brain and modify its chemical output. A few, such as thujone, one of the main terpenes in wormwood (which is used to make absinthe), bind weakly to the CB1 receptor. Others may alter the permeability of cell membranes or the blood brain-barrier, and allow in either more or less THC. Others affect serotonin and dopamine chemistry, by shutting off their production, affecting their movement, binding to their receptor sites, or slowing their natural destruction. Dopamine and serotonin, two of the main regulators of mood and attitude, are affected by some terpenes.

By temporarily altering brain function, terpenes can affect mood, sensitivity, and perception of the senses as well as bodily perceptions such as balance and pain. When terpenes are mixed, as they are in natural plant oils, they each play a role in affecting brain function. Some combinations may work synergistically and others antagonistically, but each "recipe" of terpenes affects moods and feelings in its own way.

Over 100 terpenes have been identified in marijuana. There are actually many more when one considers the multiple variations of each terpene. For instance, the characteristic citrus odor found in fruit rinds differs by type and even variety of fruit—oranges and lemons have different odors, and their terpenes—called limonenes—are mirror versions of each other. Even different varieties of oranges differ in their distinct odor. This is due to slight differences in the amounts of or form of limonene, as well as other compounds that have citrus elements.

About 10-29 percent of marijuana smoke resin is composed of terpenes. Some terpenes present in marijuana appear only occasionally in samples while others are found all the time. The percentage of terpenes and the ratios in which they are found vary by plant variety. You can experience this yourself as different varieties have different smells, indicating a different essential oil makeup.

Age, maturation and time of day of collection can affect the amount and perhaps ratios of terpenes. As plants mature, their odor gets more intense and often changes as they ripen. Climate and weather also affect terpene and flavonoid production. The same variety produces different quantities and perhaps different oils when grown in different soils or with different fertilizers.

Terpenes are constantly being produced but they evaporate under pressure from sunlight and rising temperatures. Plants have more terpenes at the end of the dark period than after a full day of light. You can test this yourself. Check a plant's odor early in the morning and at the end of a sunny day. You will find more pungency early in the morning.

Hops and both groups of *Cannabis*, low THC hemp and marijuana, contain similar complements of terpenes. One researcher found that the oil of common black pepper (*piper nigrum)* has a similar group of terpenes as *Cannabis.* Terpenes are produced in the trichomes, the same glands where THC is produced. They comprise between 10 and 20 percent of the total oils produced by the glands.

The most abundant terpenes in marijuana are described below in general order of abundance. Individual samples may differ widely, both in total percentages of terpenes and in their ratios.

Myrcene is the most prevalent terpene found in most varieties of marijuana but not found in hemp. It is also present in high amounts in hops, lemon grass, West Indian bay tree (used to make bay rum), verbena and the plant from which it derives its name, *mercia.* Myrcene appears in small amounts in the essential oils of many other plants.

Its odor is variously described as clove-like, earthy, green-vegetative, citrus, fruity with tropical mango* and minty nuances. The various odors are the result of slight differences in the overall essential oil makeup. All of these flavors and odors are commonly

* In fact, Myrcene is found in large quantities in Cavalo, Rosa, Espada and Paulista mangos.

used to describe cannabis.

Myrcene is a potent analgesic, anti-inflammatory and antibiotic. It blocks the actions of cytochrome, aflatoxin B and other pro-mutagens that are implicated in carcinogenesis. It is present in small amounts in many essential oils associated with anti-depressive and uplifting behavior.

Myrcene is probably a synergist of THC: A combination of the two molecules creates a stronger experience than THC alone. Myrcene probably affects the permeability of the cell membrane, thus it may allow more THC to reach brain cells.

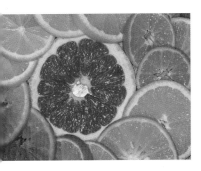

Limonene is found in the rind of citrus and many other fruits and flowers. It is the second, third or fourth most prevalent terpene in cannabis resins. Everyone is familiar with the odor of citrus resins. They explode into the air when a fruit is peeled. The exact odor is determined by the structure of the terpene.

Limonene has anti-bacterial, anti-fungal and anti-cancer activities. It inhibits the *Ras* cancer gene cascade, which promotes tumor growth. It is used to synergistically promote the absorption of other terpenes by penetrating cell membranes. Limonene sprays are used to treat depression.

Since limonene is such a potent anti-fungal and anti-cancer agent, it is thought to protect against the *Aspergillus* fungi and carcinogens found in cannabis smoke streams.

Plants use limonene to repulse predators. For instance, flies have a group of receptors similar in function to the taste buds on our tongues. One of them detects noxious chemicals, and responds to limonene as if it were toxic. It is wired directly to the fly brain.

In humans, limonene's design facilitates a direct response by quickly permeating the blood-brain barrier. The result is increased systolic blood pressure. In one test, participants reported subjective alertness and restlessness. Various limonene analogs can cue the brain to sexuality, buoyancy or focused attention.

Caryophyllene is a major terpene found in black pepper (15-25%), clove (10-20%) and cotton (15-25%). It is found in smaller percentages in many other herbs and spices. It has a sweet, woody and dry clove odor and tastes pepper spicy with camphor and astringent citrus backgrounds. It contributes to black pepper's spiciness. The oil is used industrially to enhance tobacco flavor.

Caryophyllene, given in high amounts, is a calcium and potassium ion channel blocker. As a result, it impedes the pressure exerted by heart muscles. As a topical it is analgesic and is one of the active constituents that makes clove oil, a preferred treatment for toothache.

It does not seem to be involved in mood change.

Pinene is the familiar odor associated with pine trees and their resins. It is the major component in turpentine and is found in many other plant essential oils in noticeable amounts including rosemary, sage and eucalyptus. Many additional plant oils contain minute quantities of pinene.

Pinene is used medically as an expectorant and topical antiseptic. It easily crosses the blood-brain barrier where it acts as an acetylcholinesterase inhibitor; that is, it inhibits activity of a chemical that destroys an information transfer molecule. This results in better memory. Largely due to the presence of pinene, rosemary and sage are both considered "memory plants." Concoctions made from their leaves have been used for thousands of years in traditional medicine to retain and restore memory.

Pinene probably gives true skunk varieties, the ones that stink like the animal, much of their odor. It is also a bronchodilator. The smoke seems to expand in your lungs and the high comes on very quickly since a high percentage of the substance will pass into the bloodstream and brain. It also increases focus, self-satisfaction and energy, which seems counterintuitive, but for the presence of terpineol.

Terpineol has a lilac, citrus or apple blossom/lime odor. It is a minor constituent of many plant essential oils. It is used in perfumes and soaps for fragrance.

Terpineol is obtained commercially from processing other terpenes. It reduces motility—the capability for movement—by 45% in rat tests. This may account for the couch-lock effects of some cannabis although that odor is not usually associated with body highs. However, terpineol is often found in cannabis with high pinene levels. Its odor would be masked by the pungent woodsy aromas of pinene.

Borneol smells much like the menthol aroma of camphor and is easily converted into it. It is found in small quantities in many essential oils. Commercially, it is derived from *artemisia* plants such as wormwood and some species of cinnamon.

It is considered a "calming sedative" in Chinese medicine. It is directed for fatigue, recovery from illness and stress.

The camphor-like overtones of Silver Haze varieties are unmistakable. The high does have a calming effect as well as its psychedelic aspects. This probably means that there is a large amount of borneol present.

Delta 3-Carene has a sweet pungent odor. It is a constituent of pine and cedar resin but is found in many other plants including rosemary. In aromatherapy, cypress oil, high in D-3-Carene, is used to dry excess fluids, tears, running noses, excess menstrual flow and perspiration. It may contribute to the dry eye and dry mouth experienced by marijuana users.

Linalool has a floral scent reminiscent of spring flowers such as lily of the valley, but with spicy overtones. It is refined from lavender, neroli and other essential oils. Humans can detect its odor at rates as low as one part per million in the air.

Linalool is being tested now for treatment of several types of cancers. It is also a component of several sedating essential oils. In tests on humans who inhaled it, it caused severe sedation. In tests on rats, it reduced their activity by almost 75 percent.

Pulegone has a minty-camphor odor and flavor that is used in the candy industry. It is implicated in liver damage when used in very high dosages. It is found in tiny quantities in marijuana.

Pulegone is an acetylcholinesterase inhibitor. That is, it stops the action of the protein that destroys acetylcholine, which is used by the brain to store memories. It may counteract THC's activity, which leads to low acetylcholine levels. The result is that you'd forget more on THC alone than THC accompanied by pulegone.

1,8-Cineole is the main ingredient in oil of eucalyptus. It has a camphor-minty odor. It is also found in other fragrant plants and in minor amounts in marijuana. It is used to increase circulation, pain relief and has other topical uses.

Cineole easily crosses the blood-brain-barrier and triggers a fast olfactory reaction. Eucalyptus oil is considered centering, balancing and stimulating. It is probably the stimulating and thought provoking part of the cannabis smoke stream.

Terpenes and their interactions with each other and resultant effect on brain activities is a fascinating territory, and another level of exploration and creativity for seed breeders. By learning the odors of the terpenes, you may be able to predict the mind-altering properties each lends to a bud.

KC-36

KC Brains

K C-36 is a mostly indica strain that is a great choice for outdoor grow-ers in temperate regions. This strain was bred specifically to thrive at high latitudes. It flourishes indoors or out, and can be grown in Holland or at equivalent distances from the equator with a finishing time at the end of September. In fact, it will flower too early if attempted outdoors in more southerly latitudes.

As an indoor plant, KC-36 finishes in eight to ten weeks. She stays small and compact, making her great for indoor growers with space lim-itations. Outdoors, KC-36 will reach moderate heights, around 5-6 feet (1.75 to 2 m). KC Brains recommends growing in hydro indoors but suggests that outdoor grows in soil should consider organics in order to allow the buds to bring their best qualities forward in the harvest.

KC-36 shows her strong indica influence in her wide, webbed, dark green leaves; in her bushy stature, and eventually, in her dense and compact buds, profuse with crystal forma-tions like the signature frost of her White Widow mother. She is a multi-brancher, with tight buds forming in many locations. She tends to have an asymmetrical profile because some of her branches stick out.

This vigorous northern plant can adjust to variable weather conditions and withstands both cold weather and moisture in moderate doses. She has shown some mold resistance when faced with wet conditions. KC-36 is also quite smelly, which may be a disadvantage if countermeasures are not in place or the outdoor location is not remote enough from curious neighbors.

KC-36 has a fast-onset, powerful body high. The inhale is expansive, with a floral spice reminiscent of White Widow. Its smoke is likely to cause little coughing spells, followed by smiles and body relaxation. This is more of a cozy afternoon smoke than a party pot. KC recommends it for a lazy day of hanging with friends, for an enhanced sense of peace when out in nature, or as a nice enhancement for a good movie or CD. Anecdotally, it's good medicine for migraines and hyperactivity.

 85I/15S

 cozy, body stone

 floral

 56-70 days; end Sept.

 White Widow ♀ X KC 606 ♂

 1 g/ watt of light in; .75-1.25 kg out

 SOG

KC-45

KC Brains

Photos: Ed Rosenthal

The KC-45 is an unusual variety among the many selections on the market due to her partial ruderalis heritage. Ruderalis is a distinct Russian subspecies of cannabis whose most notable characteristic is auto-flowering. Unlike indica and sativa strains, ruderalis is not triggered into flowering based on the number of hours of darkness. Ruderalis begins flowering automatically after growing to a certain age, even outdoors in her native Russia. KC's ruderalis-sativa hybrid, KC-45, bounces back from stress conditions and can perform in cloudy weather due to its ruderalis mother's minimal need for externally triggered flowering. Meanwhile, its sativa father ensures a strong, euphoric high.

While KC-45 can be grown under lights, it is more appropriate for outdoor gardens. This multi-branched plant grows best in soil, especially with an organic fertilizing program. Once it roots, KC-45 will grow to a nearly 7-foot-tall Christmas tree, whose impressively long branches remain bare of leaves near the stem, but support meter-long colas. In outdoor environments, this plant will ripen by September 15; indoors, it takes 8-10 weeks to finish flowering.

Indoor plants are very high yielders, and outdoor yields can weigh in at over 3 pounds per plant. The buds that form are long and cylindrical. The colas are compact but not tight, because the individual flowers that make up the cola are slender rather than plump.

The smell from this plant is localized, but will burst with a strong lemon odor when touched. When smoked, the KC-45 high comes on rapid and strong. It retains the uplifting stone of its Brazilian sativa parentage, but modified a bit by the ruderalis, making this smoke less hyper than a pure sativa. The result is an energetic yet calm and settling high, well suited to gardening, hiking or leisurely sports. Medicinally, this variety has provided relief to some migraine sufferers and also is good for any condition which causes lethargy, as it can improve energy levels.

 50 Sativa/50 Ruderalis

 energetic but calm

 very lemony

 56-70 days/mid-Sept.

 russian ruderalis ♀ X brazilian sativa ♂

 high indoor yield 1.5 kg/plant out

 SOG

Kish

Cash Crop Ken

Photos: Boyscout

In the language of pot breeding, "berry" strains are usually dark, strong indicas with sweet flavors. Kish is a cross of two Shishkaberries, which are themselves a Blueberry/Stinky Afghan cross, noted for their cherry-flavored smoke. Thus Kish is very, very "berry"—tasty, potent, and easy to grow; a great candidate for the beginning cultivator who wants a classic couch-lock high.

This indica-dominant plant grows short and bushy, like a miniature Christmas tree with broad leaves and one primary cola. If the top is cropped, Kish will umbrella. However, Kish likes her main cola, and if side branches are trimmed this plant will happily invest its energy in the single bud, making it great for sea of green systems.

A quick finisher, Kish can be ready for harvest in as few as 6 weeks of flowering depending on the intensity of sun or lights that shine on your garden. In fact, allowing it to ripen for 7 weeks or more results in a reduction in the quality of the harvest. Kish does better under Sunmasters than HPS lights. When budded in big pots, this strain will usually reach 3-4 feet in height at finish. Yields have been reported at around 56 g per plant. It can also grow outdoors with good results. It will finish by the end of September.

Along with the fast finish, Kish is likely to be successful for the starting garden because it is a versatile plant, proving hardy in many grow environments, and showing great stamina when faced with stresses. The harvest-ready buds are deserving of the name "nugget." They are round, chunky and surprisingly hard. The buds shrink very little when drying, meaning that each cola really weighs in. Kish buds have a sharp fruity flavor, leaning toward cherry or raspberry. Kish is strong in buzz as well as taste. Two or three tokes will knock even a seasoned smoker between the eyes. Although not too sleepy, this buzz tends to be low tempo, with good duration, and is probably best suited for armchair olympics, with snacks near at hand. This variety is a favorite among multiple sclerosis patients.

3rd place, *Cannabis Culture* Toker's Bowl 2004, 4th place, *Cannabis Culture* Toker's Bowl 2005

 mostly indica

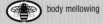 body mellowing

 sharp, fruity

 42-45 days

 Shiskaberry x Shiskaberry

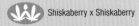 Up to 2-4 oz./plant in, more out

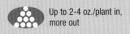

 SOG

Kiwiskunk

Kiwiseeds

 75I/25S

 stoney

 sweet, citrus

 50-60 days

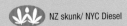 NZ skunk/ NYC Diesel

 400-500 g/m²

 SOG

In the late 1980s the skunk invasion landed on New Zealand's shores. This short-flowering, heavy-yielding variety added a whole new dimension to growing in New Zealand, which at that stage was limited to outdoor guerrilla groves of big sativas. Smaller indica-dominant plants meant less chance of detection by air; earlier flowering meant valuable crops were in before drug enforcement agencies spotted them, and the novelty of the skunk stone meant prices for the herb were higher than for the traditional sativas. Hence many haze/sativa growers around that time gave up their long-flowering types for indica, stabilizing unique strains of New Zealand ("kiwi") skunk. Kiwiskunk is a cross of one of these skunks with a NYC Diesel, adding something extra when it comes to taste.

All the classic skunk qualities are here: short and stocky plants, high calyx-to-leaf ratio, full fat buds, and excellent yields. The strain also boasts superior mold resistance, making her an attractive choice for both new and veteran growers, indoors or out.

Perfect for sea of green cultivation styles, Kiwiskunk will be ready to harvest within 8½ weeks of flowering. Growers can expect yields of around 400-500 grams (14-18 oz.) per square meter when grown SOG style, and a little more if she is given an extra week or two of vegetative growth. This strain's exceptional consistency makes Kiwiskunk a good choice for small growers who want to crop her as soon as possible, rather than waiting to grow out and select the best females.

Kiwiskunk's package of qualities includes the distinct skunk smell! Without some form of smell suppression you'll run the risk of the neighbors knowing your business. Growers in the Netherlands use carbon filters for this plant—taking the same precautions as they would if growing NYC Diesel, which has a reputation for getting growers into trouble with the smell she emits.

Kiwiskunk has a great skunky taste with a touch of citrus. The smoke is sweet and bright—a light inhale. Don't be fooled. This skunk packs a punch! A bowl of Kiwiskunk will drop you into a deep stone with giggles inside it, best enjoyed from a sofa in front of a big screen movie.

Kiwiseeds History

Kiwiseeds was started in 2001 by two New Zealand brothers with a long-time passion for marijuana. The family business had always been growing plants of one kind or another, and the two boys grew up alongside a whole array of crops from cut-flowers to strawberries, from tomatoes to commercial forest plantations. Among all this family horticulture, the boys acquired their first cannabis seeds from an older friend at the tender age of 10 or 11. They hadn't even tried smoking cannabis, but when they grew the seeds, the plants were not only beautiful, but their mystique was thrilling and irresistible.

The boys grew up, their plants grew up, and so did their reputation as competent growers. The skills learned from their family business were really starting to pay off. When they left school at the tender age of 15, they were already teaching some of the old-school growers how best to cultivate cannabis. Before long their services as advisors to growers were becoming more and more in demand.

facing prosecution for growing or possessing cannabis. They now go about their work, quietly doing what they know best—producing great cannabis for everyone to enjoy.

In 2006 Kiwiseeds joined up with the renowned Dampkring coffeeshop to start the Dampkring Growshop, situated opposite the Central Station, right in the heart of Amsterdam. If you make it to this colorful city, stop by!

In the mid-1980s the brothers were given 10 large Cannonball seeds by a good friend returning from the USA's West Coast. This was the first time they had grown out a fat, skunk-type indica. Crossing these fat-leafed skunks with the typical thin-leafed, sativa-dominant, long flowering strains endemic to New Zealand became a whole new hobby. The lads had found a breeding niche that increased their passion for pot horticulture.

Dampkring Growshop
11 Prins Hendrikkade
Amsterdam

In the early 1990s the brothers arrived in Holland on a mission to acquire more skunk varieties and Dutch hybrids. Over the next few years, they traveled frequently between New Zealand and Holland, until settling in Amsterdam for good in 1993.

Since then things have gone from good to better for the two brothers. Several of their varieties have gained popularity in Holland's coffeeshops. Their company name, "Kiwiseeds," is intended as a tribute to New Zealand, the country that gave them the chance to get where they are, but also as a bit of a dig at that country's cannabis policies. In Holland, the Kiwiseeds duo no longer spend half their life in court,

Kushage

TH Seeds

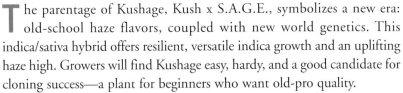

The parentage of Kushage, Kush x S.A.G.E., symbolizes a new era: old-school haze flavors, coupled with new world genetics. This indica/sativa hybrid offers resilient, versatile indica growth and an uplifting haze high. Growers will find Kushage easy, hardy, and a good candidate for cloning success—a plant for beginners who want old-pro quality.

This plant does amazingly well in places that are prone to powdery mildew. Just like her mother, she will be the last plant in the room to go down if left unwatered. When forced to flower at one foot (30 cm), Kushage will finish at 4.5 to 5 feet (140-160 cm). In sea of green gardens, plants deliver 25-40 grams ($^3/_4$ to $1^1/_2$ ounces) each. In one-gallon buckets, the yields per plant can increase up to 2 ounces (60 g). Larger plants in 5-gallon buckets produce 55-100 g (2-$3^1/_2$ ounces). When grown indoors, Kushage finishes in $10^1/_2$ weeks. TH Seeds recommends hydro methods for biggest yield, or soil for the most succulent flavors. Like many mindful cultivators, TH Seeds recommends organic fertilizers for all gardeners.

Kushage starts off very straight, branches a lot, and tends to lean as she matures. It's a good idea to cut off the lower third of her branches to let the others breathe. Her first leaves are very wide, but subsequent leaves skinny up as the plant grows. They are waxy, and much darker than her buds, which are lime green, resembling her S.A.G.E. father. The large calyxes come from her Kush mother. Kushage buds are spade-shaped and frosty with fresh-smelling resin, giving the ripe colas a spiky or jewelry-like appearance.

If flowered soon after cloning, Kushage produces a single large cola with a rock-hard crown of lower buds. Kushage's buds retain their pine fresh scent as they dry and a spicy undertone that comes out when burned. This strain's sativa-dominant high is a great mind opener for brainstorms, conceptualizing, or creating artwork. It is less favorable when efficiency or punctuality is on the agenda. Medical patients have found this strain helpful for relieving the symptoms of multiple sclerosis.

3rd Prize, *High Times* Cannabis Cup (sativa category) 2005

 S I 60S/40I

 quick, mind-expanding

 fresh, piney

 75 days

 OGer Kush from L.A. ♀ x S.A.G.E. ♂

 SOG: 25-40 g plantlets; 35-100 g/plant in

 SOG

LA Confidential

DNA Genetics

L A Confidential is a commercial seed strain that captures the genetics of OG Kush. An Afghan strain grown from clones, OG Kush first became popular in the Los Angeles market in the 1990s, and then became world famous as California rappers like Snoop Dogg, Method Man and Cypress Hill namechecked it in their songs. OG Kush offered a hash-like experience from reefer: a resinous smoke, deep and spicy-sweet like nutmeg, that drew the smoker into a lush, slightly trippy dreamland. While "Authentic OG Kush" may be hard to find if you're not a rap star, DNA's LA Confidential brings the secrets of this celebrity smoke to the market.

LA Confidential is an indoor-adapted plant that can also be grown outdoors or in a greenhouse. This strain is resistant to mildew, and on the whole is easy for even a novice to grow. She likes any medium—hydro, coco beds, soil, or NFT systems. If forced into flowering at 3-4 feet of growth (about 1m), LA Confidential stays petite, gaining only a foot (30cm) in the rest of her cycle, making her a good strain for gardeners with limited space. DNA themselves prefer bigger plants, vegetated for 3-4 weeks, for a lower overall plant count. Like many eco-conscious growers, DNA recommends organic nutrients.

As she moves through flowering, LA Confidential forms popcorn-like buds that are very dense, and so dark green that they almost appear black by harvest time. The flowering time is speedy, finishing in 7-8 weeks indoors, or by late September to early October when grown outside. These are the sweet "rocks" of resinous bud associated with her OG Kush ancestors. LA Confidential is not the biggest yielding strain, with average yields between 300-500 grams per square meter from "petite" plants in close quarters; yields from larger or outdoor plants may be correspondingly greater.

LA Confidential delivers a heavy "Kush" high: tasty, languorous, and a little psychedelic. Experienced smokers will find it relaxing but not sleepy, although probably too relax-

 100% indica

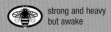 strong and heavy but awake

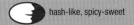 hash-like, spicy-sweet

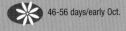 46-56 days/early Oct.

 California indica ♀ x Afghan indica ♂

300-500 g/m²

greenhouse

ing if there are complex tasks to be done. This is a chill-out smoke. What this strain lacks in monstrous yields it makes up for in high, taste, and smell. Many weed experts agree—LA Confidential has won second (2005) and third (2004) place for indica at the *High Times* Cannabis Cup, and first place for indica in the *International Cannagraphics* Cup (2005).

Lowryder #2

High Bred Seeds

The long-awaited successor to the Joint Doctor's flagship strain is finally ready for your garden. Lowryder #2 is the newest development in High Bred Seed's quest to improve the strength, yield and flavor of the original Lowryder variety while maintaining the unusual characteristics that made this compact plant so popular.

Lowryder #2 is the second "dwarf" plant from Joint Doctor. This version is infused with superior Santa Maria genetics. The result is an auto-flowering dwarf that yields a wonderfully strong, head-turning sandalwood smoke with an earthy, rich taste. Besides strength and flavor, this strain boasts copious resin production and much-improved yield and stability. Her buds are larger, tighter and more aromatic than buds from the original strain of the same name.

This new cross was selectively inbred for three generations to ensure 100% auto-flowering, which derives from vestigial bits of Mexican-acclimated ruderalis genetics somewhere in her ancient history. Lowryder #2 is virtually "programmed" to begin flowering at 3 weeks, but the rapidity of her growth cycle can vary according to the intensity of light. As with the original Lowryder, no separate room or change of light cycle is needed to flower Lowryder #2. She finishes from seed to harvest in 2 months flat when given 14 hours of daylight per day.

Lowryder #2 branches a lot at the base, especially if topped at a young age. She responds well to moderate feedings, does not stretch, and seems particularly well adapted to indoor settings. Because Lowryder #2 does not require a long dark period in order to maintain flowering, she can be given up to 18 hours of light in the flowering phase, resulting in faster growth. This strain also matures faster than most non-auto-flowering varieties when grown outdoors in moderate climates. Although the breeder does not mention it, the autoflowering of this variety is due to a partial ruderalis ancestry. She is also suitable for tem-

 mostly indica

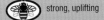 strong, uplifting

 sandalwood

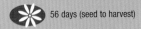 56 days (seed to harvest)

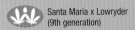 Santa Maria x Lowryder (9th generation)

 ½ oz./plant

 SOG

perate to Nordic climates and performs well in locations with short seasons.

Like the original Lowryder, this plant can be grown as bonsai cannabis. The average height of Lowryder #2 is 10-16 inches (25-40 cm), with yields around $^1/_2$ ounce of resinous bud per plant. Her miniature size makes camouflage easy, while also allowing growers to garden in locations like windowboxes, patios, grow boxes, or closets, in addition to more standard garden setups. These plants do well as a sea of green.

Lowryder #2 has been dubbed "pot for dummies." This strain attracts many first-time growers because of her ease, speed, stealth, and stone: a strong and unusually uplifting indica high.

Kiwiseeds

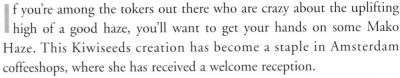

 75S/25I

 full head high

 earthy/spicy

 70-90 days

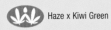 Haze x Kiwi Green

 550-650 g/m²

I f you're among the tokers out there who are crazy about the uplifting high of a good haze, you'll want to get your hands on some Mako Haze. This Kiwiseeds creation has become a staple in Amsterdam coffeeshops, where she has received a welcome reception.

The name comes from the Mako shark, an extremely powerful and beautiful creature that frequents the southern latitudes. As one of the fastest fish in the ocean, this ferocious shark can attain swimming speeds of up to 35 kilometers per hour and can leap clear of the water to heights of up to 6 meters. Kiwiseeds named their new strain Mako Haze because of her speed and strength and her ability to literally stun her users.

There's only a touch of indica in Mako Haze's breeding. As such, she exhibits strong sativa growth habits: elongated branches and dense clusters of flowers that are sticky with resin. This plant grows best in large pots with plenty of room to stretch out. The breeders recommend 9 plants per square meter as the perfect configuration. Any greater density, and the growing area can become a jungle.

Plants can be "tipped" during the growing stage for best results. Kiwiseeds gardeners usually tip pots to an angle twice during the growing cycle: once early in the growing stage (3rd or 4th set of leaves) then again one week into flowering. This encourages the plant to form an even set of 6 buds instead of one main cola.

Sativas require more patient gardeners. This variety requires 10-13 weeks to reach peak ripeness, but huge yields of quality smoking material can be expected. When dry, the THC crystals are so thick they almost look matted together.

In 2005, Kiwiseeds had the Mako Haze analyzed by experts for THC content. The result of 19.7% staggered even her breeders. Her smoke is lovely and smooth, with a heavy hazy taste, and her high is up, up, up! Haze strains like the Mako have a therapeutic effect on mental states and are good treatments for lethargy and depression.

1st Prize, 2006 *High Times* Cannabis Cup, Best Sativa category.

Martian Mean Green

DNA Genetics

Martian Mean Green's mother is a resinous, stable cross of Great White Shark and the notorious Rastafarian reefer, Jamaican Lamb's Bread. The papa comes from the deepest roots of the seed business—Neville is the man who in the late 1980s brought the Real G13 to his "C" Haze male, which is one of the major building blocks for many of the haze strains today.

Martian Mean Green is a hybrid indica/sativa with a slight leaning toward the sativa side. This combination makes for a haze-like smoke with an upbeat but not harsh or speedy stone. This variety has yet to be tested in an outdoor grow, but indoors, she takes 9-10 weeks to finish. Outdoor and greenhouse cultivation should also work well with this versatile strain.

The strength of this variety is that she will grow well under heat, and thrive in the cold. DNA Genetics prefers to grow organically in soil, and tries to spread the good word about the quality of organic grows. It is possible for the beginner to get a connoisseur grow on the first time out with Martian Mean Green. However, fertilizers are a matter of personal choice, just be sure to flush plants in the last few weeks of flowering.

Martian Mean Green averages 3 feet (1m) of height at the beginning of flowering, and usually adds only 1-2 feet (30-60 cm) before finishing. Average yields are in the neighborhood of 100 grams per plant. If you want to avoid a 3-4 week vegetative period and instead plant 20-25 plants per square meter, yields will be around 400-600 grams per square meter. Her buds look fairly loose in formation, but upon further inspection are not as loose as many typical sativas.

As this dark green plant moves from the vegetative to the flowering phase, her piney smell graduates from noticeable to really stinking up the place. Martian Mean Green's mega-smell is out of this world and definitely requires distant neighbors and precautionary measures.

 60S/40I

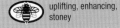 uplifting, enhancing, stoney

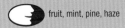 fruit, mint, pine, haze

 63-70 days

 Sharksbreath ♀ x G-13 Haze ♂

 400-600 g/m²

 greenhouse

 SOG

When smoked, her intense odor—fruity sweet, minty and piney, with a distinct haze edge—refreshes your senses, while her strong instant rush achieves flying saucer escape velocity. The Martian is a power stone—a fast start followed by a long sustained high. Once in orbit, you will find yourself supremely stoned yet not sleepy, seeing life on earth as a cartoon filled with silly insights and unex-pected laughs. No paranoia here—this strain is recom-mended for relief of anxiety and stress. Martian weed has no burn-out factor, making it a steady companion over time.

Best Seed Company Sativa, *High Times* Cannabis Cup 2005

Motavation

Magus Genetics

Photo: Mosca Negra

Motavation may seem like an ironic name for this highly relaxing couch-lock strain, but the quality it calls to mind, one stoners are stereotyped for lacking, is not its origin. It is instead named for a favorite band of the Magus Genetics crew (see next page), a band who named themselves for *mota*, the Spanish word for pot. This strong indica will "*mota*-vate" smokers to put up their feet and take it easy for a while.

This strain's indica/sativa mix can only be estimated since both parents have an uncertain or "top secret" ancestry, but Motavation's stone and appearance confirm her indica-dominant genetics. Short and squat, this plant is a little leafy and shows moderate stretching at flowering. The copious resin on her leafy matter may put you in the mind to become more earth friendly and "recycle."

This indoor plant is best suited as a multi-branch grower. Her lateral growth is strong, sometimes even equalling growth on the main stem. Sea of green cultivation is also possible, using a short vegetative time. When vegetated for 4-5 weeks, plants will reach approximately $2^1/_2$ feet (80 cm) and yield about 80 grams apiece.

Motavation buds will mostly be firm but not rock hard. Her leaves are a thick, dark green. A reddish purple coloration often emerges at the end of the flowering cycle, especially when plants have been exposed to low temperatures. As with most plants, her yield is reduced if low temperatures have been the norm throughout the cycle.

Motavation's odor is strong and penetrating with a touch of petrochemical, like turpentine or fresh paint. The flavor is much softer and richer, a strong complexity of carbon and sweetness like sweet tobacco or raisins. The high starts in the head, as your thoughts wander off, soon followed by a deeply relaxing but not necessarily soporific body stone. The reduction of tension may be just what some people need to drift off, but even if it doesn't make your eyes droop, it is not really a sensible "day smoke" choice. This variety may leave you couch-locked and lost in your own thoughts. While it may awaken some interesting connections and inspire you, it is unlikely that you will be motivated to act on them until the *mota* has worn off.

 30S/70I

 quick head high/physical, possible couchlock

carbon, sweetness

 50-60 days

 Sensi Star, M.I., Holland ♀/ Warlock, M.I., Holland ♂

 80 g/plant

 less desirable

Behind the Motavation

Motavation—the Band

The members of Motavation have been immersed in the Blues from Chicago's Maxwell Street Flea Market music scene since they were kids.

The band met one Sunday night at an open mike jam near Chicago. Their similar musical interests in Chicago's Electric Blues, better known as Maxwell Street Blues, inspired them to form Motavation. Strong Blues Shuffle and Swing Blues rhythmic influences are the basis for their music.

The members of this band found that *mota*—Spanish for "pot"—was also a shared interest. Like many musicians, they used pot to explore the world of music, and socially to bond and connect as a band. Hence the name Motavation (Music Motivated by Mota). More information about Motavation can be found at www.motavation.nl.

Motavation—the Strain

At the end of 1999 Sensi Star and Warlock were the two most popular strains on Amsterdam's Bluebird coffeeshop menu. Magus Genetics had started selling Warlock seeds the year before, and the Bluebird had been carrying Warlock on their menu, on and off, since 1993.

The folks at Bluebird asked Magus's breeder if he would crossbreed Warlock with Sensi Star and select a new "Bluebird Exclusive" from the offspring. As it happened, he already had a seed crop planned at that time, so it was no trouble to add their favorite Sensi Star clone to the room that was going to be pollinated by the Warlock male. About one year later when Magus had grown out a handful of seedlings from this cross, only one possessed a truly balanced combination of Sensi Star and Warlock characteristics that the Bluebird was looking for. After

being propogated, this cross was added to the Bluebird menu as "Starwarz."

Other plants from this cross had desirable characteristics from both sides—a Sensi Star-dominant growing pattern and a Warlock bud structure. Their aroma was different, though. They didn't have the mixed sweetness of the Starwarz, but had a somewhat sharp turpentine aroma, with the Sensi Star's sweetness as an undertone.

Although the job for Bluebird was finished, breeding is an ongoing quest. Magus kept the Sensi Star mother clone for future experiments. After receiving some more Sensi Star seeds from a friend, Magus decided to start an inbred line from the clone, and to see if they could produce a reasonably consistent hybrid representing the "turpentine" phenotype.

This project went very well. Even the transitional testcrosses between Starwarz and the definitive Motavation were well received by growers. One of them built a name for itself in Austria, where it was known as "Medizin Power." At the end of 2004, the best-performing Motavation line was selected for reproduction, and the remaining seeds of that family where given away as freebees at the first London Hemp Fair under the name "London Memories."

Mother's Finest

Sensi Seed Bank

Photos: Perhaps

 75S/25I

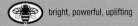 bright, powerful, uplifting

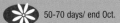 sweet + haze tang

 50-70 days/ end Oct.

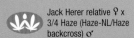 Jack Herer relative ♀ x 3/4 Haze (Haze-NL/Haze backcross) ♂

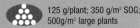 125 g/plant; 350 g/m² SOG; 500g/m² large plants

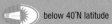 below 40°N latitude

 SOG

Mother's Finest is an uplifting sativa-dominant ganja that loves to grow. This homebody prefers the great indoors, but she can grow in all regions of the southern hemisphere or in warm sunny climates below 40 degrees North latitude.

Mother's Finest can be vegetated to fill a whole room or cage with a single plant, a boon for growers with plant number limitations. Almost any size is possible; expect an increase in height by a factor of three to five during flowering. With a starting size of 12-16 inches (30-40 cm), the typical finishing size (although not the maximum) is 4¹/₂ to 5¹/₄ feet (140-160 cm). Some phenotypes express the strain's subdued indica background, finishing significantly faster. These plants will still gain a lot of height as they flower.

Mother's Finest is great for training or super-cropping. Keeping these plants short (which enables sea of green cultivation) is possible with a little care. In order to do so, clones need to be flowered as soon as they root (4-6 in./10-15 cm). Flowering within a few days of pruning can keep replacement stems compact, but won't stop them from appearing. This strain's branches have a strong, distinctly upward slant, like a poplar. Her long, firm stems root easily, which is great for cloning; mother plants can be re-used for years.

This variety stays green and healthy with a lower than usual dose of hydro nutrient. She is not as sensitive as some sativas, but definitely not as nutrient-hungry as a straight indica. She finishes in 7-10 weeks; most phenotypes require 9 weeks or more for full maturity. Indoor plant yields average 500 grams per square meters in gardens with reasonable ceiling heights. SOG yields are closer to 350 grams per square meter.

In addition to the impressive lengths that the branches and buds can reach on this variety, growers will be amazed with the amount of resin glands smothering them. The dense sticky covering along with the sparseness of the slender light green leaves make this plant less hospitable to spider mites, who can't walk on this surface or spin their unwelcome webs.

Her buds are spears with small peaks of calyxes growing outward in all directions, which gives them a wicked "horned" or fractal appearance. For a sativa influenced plant, the buds are suprising in their weight and density. The pale pistils darken to shades of light-orange, gold, yellow and even pink when mature. Well-grown Mother's Finest does not produce feathery or fluffy buds —an extra-high resin content keeps flowers brittle after drying. Her resin glands often stay clear and light-refracting right up to harvest, so growers who examine trichomes to judge maturity should look to the fullness of the gland-heads, rather than the proportion of cloudy or amber trichomes.

Mother's Finest produces little odor while growing, and only begins to smell sharply when dried—a haze tang combined with a sweet, fruity body and an undertone of skunk. The whiff of haze that teases in the aroma will deliver in the high. Its bright, powerful and uplifting mental chime can be maintained for hours with careful toking. If the pipe is set down for a while, the smoker can expect a smooth descent into a chilled, sociable vibe. Mother's Finest is a great daytime smoke, suitable for conversation, partying or running errands in a magically enhanced world.

First Place, *High Times* Cannabis Cup, Sativa category 2002

Mother's Finest

Mother's Finest isn't talking about anyone's mom. She was named for the Mothers of Invention, the band formed by the irreverent and energetic genius Frank Zappa. With more than one serious Zappa fan in the Sensi family, many names were bandied about to honor him. Naming a plant after Frank himself didn't seem appropriate, as he didn't seem to like cannabis much more than any other drug—which is to say not at all. But we can be fairly sure that the Mothers enjoyed their herb.

Mother's Finest is an interesting offshoot of the Jack Herer breeding program, retaining as much indica weight and density as possible, while concentrating the sharp haze high. Just as Jack Flash is a descendent of Jack Herer, which follows a bulkier, stonier, skunkier line, Mother's Finest follows a decidedly hazey upward path, without sacrificing the advantages of the indica balance found in Jack Herer.

Despite her strengths, Mother's Finest is not ideal for a first-time grow. Gardeners should have grown a few gardens before expecting the fantastic results that are possible with Mother's Finest. Although the sativa breeding in this variety gives her a tropical resistance to heat and humidity, she would be out of her element in temperate outdoor regions. Anyone who grows Mother's Finest should remember the basic rules for success with sativa hybrids indoors—less fertilizer, short vegetative periods and plenty of bright light.

Mount Cook

Kiwiseeds

 75I/25S

 strong body

 sweet, hashy

 50-65 days

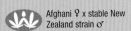 Afghani ♀ x stable New Zealand strain ♂

 500-600 g/m²

 SOG

This delightful indica-dominant hybrid was given its name as a tribute to the highest mountain in New Zealand. At 3754 meters (12,316 feet), Mount Cook dominates the Southern Alps, a mountain range that forms the backbone of the South Island. Mount Cook, known by the Maori people as Aoraki, is a majestic sight amidst one of the most beautiful landscapes in the world.

This strain's father is a stabilized New Zealand strain from the Mount Cook vicinity, while her mother was selected from Kiwiseed's best Afghani females. Her indica heritage gives Mount Cook wide and deep-green leaves, and thick stems and branches ready to support her heavy fruiting. This variety is perfect for sea of green at around 15-20 plants per square meter. She is just as happy in a 10-liter (3-gallon) pot under 18 hours of light, for a slightly longer growing period.

Mount Cook has great potential for the indoor grower. Her flowering time is reasonable, and her yields are satisfying, making this variety a great addition to any grow-room. Her fruit does tend to become rather top heavy in the last two weeks of flowering, so support of some kind is advisable. The breeders recommend using netting that allows for the tops to grow through and be supported. Netting stretches out, so it can be secured at the corners with hooks or a staple gun. Mount Cook's Afghani heritage shows in her heavy yield of snowy white buds, up to 600 grams per square meter in sea of green.

Mount Cook is a plant for indica lovers. Her buzz is heavy, almost paralyzing for the first few minutes, then it mellows out to a nice body stone that lasts for a couple of hours. This sweet hashy tasting smoke is best to share with good friends, whether spending the day sunning at the beach, or an afternoon lounging at home. However, it is definitely not one to smoke while behind the wheel of anything!

Nuken

Cash Crop Ken

 mostly indica

 deep stone, relaxing

 sweet and grassy

 49-56 days/early Oct.

 Kish x God Bud

 need

 SOG

Nuken is a Canadian native, a cross of a Kish father (see Kish) and a God Bud mother. God Bud is a beloved purple skunk strain that has gathered a reputation up north for easy growing and a deep stone. It came to Cash Crop Ken from a veteran grower of 30 years. Kish is a double Shiskaberry cross that is indica dominant, so she finishes quickly and produces a satisfying harvest of chunky nugs. She has emerged as a popular Afghan in recent years, a solid producer of resinous buds with strong effects. Coming from these parents, Nuken promises to be a real warhead of hassle-free indica meltdown.

Nuken is easier to grow and reaches larger sizes than her parents. Her height more than doubles during the flowering cycle, and can easily reach 5 feet (1.6 m) by harvest. Nuken can be pruned to a make a good sea of green plant and is also suitable as a multi-branch plant. Her branches are thick, lessening the need for support, and her seven-leaflet foliage is a medium green. Nuken is proven indoors, where she grows comfortably and ripens in a short 7-8 weeks. Although she has not yet been tested outdoors, her harvests can be expected in late September or early October. As with many Afghani strains, this plant should be kept away from moisture.

Nuken's buds are rounded and tight, although not quite as rock hard as her Kish parent. The buds are not especially smelly when growing, yet Nuken's finished smoke fills the mouth with an almost marshmallow type sweetness and a strong skunky green overtone. Her buzz is long lasting and quite strong, relaxing without being especially sleepy. It can be a good day or evening smoke, but probably not one for a work break. Nuken's indica body radiation is best for chatting, or kicking back and taking it easy with a good movie at home, or the video that glows in your own imagination.

Opium

Paradise Seeds

Photos: Trichome Pharm and Jean from France

This bittersweet 50/50 hybrid is the result of a cross between a mostly sativa mother selected for her potency and short bloom period, and a mostly indica "reversed" female "father." A versatile plant, Opium can be grown indoors, or outdoors when the region is comparable to France —warm and sunny, generally between the latitudes 50 degrees North and South. She can also be grown as a sea of green or multi-branch plant depending on how long you vegetate her.

Opium has at least one characteristic in common with its namesake, beyond the interesting flavor—a large top flower. On all of the phenotypes observed, her calyx-to-leaf ratio is very high. Huge bracts pile up on each other, all wearing fine-looking trichome coats—the biggest colas that the breeders at Paradise Seeds have ever seen. When allowed to grow as a multi-branch plant, the branches become profuse. One experienced grower respectfully calls this branchy phenotype "the totem."

When raised hydroponically or on coco, Opium performs phenomenally in terms of manageability and vigorous growth. Pruning the lower third of a well-constituted plant will ease the manicuring process and really valorize her monstrous top colas and huge surrounding bracts. Given time to mature, the final look and feel of her buds says "quality" —a pale green cured flower with a silverish sheen and subtle shades of mixed colors. Her smell is also exponentially enhanced after proper curing and can become harder to mask.

Opium's fragrance and tastes are composed mostly of fruit, although they traverse a range of exotic, terpene-induced associations. While most plants have a creamy tropical punch taste, one phenotype leans toward with a noticeably different, astringent grape taste. The "grapey" plants can often be identified by the beautiful purple and pink notes in their coloring.

 50S/50I

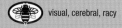 visual, cerebral, racy

 sweet and bitter fruit punch

 60 days

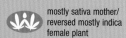 mostly sativa mother/ reversed mostly indica female plant

 550 g/m² in; + 600/plant out

 SOG

Opium is a majestic plant, with intense smoke from liftoff to landing, Opium does not leave you crashing on the ground at the end of the ride. Her sativa heritage registers in every cell of your body, lifting you up with an amazing cerebral high complete with visuals and racing thoughts. Given the right setting, she is a bright daytime smoke, although she may lead you to play hooky after lunch.

Second Place, *High Times* Cannabis Cup, Seed Bank Sativa 2006

Posh

Cash Crop Ken

 85I/15S

 stress relief, sleepy

 hashy, piney

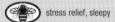 50 days/end Sept.

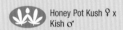 Honey Pot Kush ♀ x Kish ♂

 340 g/plant, 1000 g/m² in SOG

 SOG

Take the nuggety berry of Kish and cross it with a Honey Pot mother and Posh is what you get. This is a plant bred for good taste and a deep, stress-relieving stone.

This mostly indica hybrid grows fast, tripling in height after the flip from vegetative to flowering phase. She rises up like an evergreen tree with elongated, flexible branches that bend back, making some type of support or tying system advisable in order to maintain an even dispersal of light to the buds.

This Canada native, like its Honey Pot mother, is super easy to clone, with a fast recovery time and a good rate for success. However it is inadvisable to stress this plant. Posh is a bit finicky about her environmental conditions. This tall thin supermodel will suffer if the temperature undergoes any big changes, and may become unstable or exhibit hermaprhoditism. If she is accidentally exposed to drastic shifts in the rhythms of the grow room, the breeder advises that the main stalks be checked for pollen sacs in order to avoid accidental pollination. For this reason, Posh may be more suited to a gardener with a bit of experience in controlling conditions.

If raised right, Posh can deliver some explosive colas that compare to the size of a two-liter bottle. Yields are close to a pound per 1000 watts of light in SOG. The willowy nature of this plant makes her easy to manicure, and the buds retain enough of the nugget-like solidity of the Kish parent to weigh in for a satisfying yield. At ripeness, they often take on tinges of purple, and give off a strong pine fragrance.

The Posh buzz is devastating. Her strong head/body combo make this an ideal late night smoke. The high creeps into an intense mind-boggling sensation that is effective for disrupting persistent or cycling thoughts and giving the psyche a rest. While in daytime or active situations this might be disorienting or immobilizing, at night it can be a fantastic and smooth sendoff to slumber.

Purple Kush

Coffeeshop SR-71

This pure indica medicinal strain comes from California. In that state's medical community she is considered an "elite clone," meaning that she is only available as a cutting. Not to worry if you are a medical marijuana patient in California – this strain can be found at various dispensaries throughout the state. Purple Kush is especially popular at the SR-71 dispensary in "Oaksterdam," the section of downtown Oakland that tolerates medical marijuana providers. Patients there praise this Purple Kush's deep body stone as a treatment for pain and depression.

This lady forms a short squat bush with very dense internodes and huge fan leaves, staying in the 2-3-foot height range indoors. With topping or pinching she will be at least as wide as she is tall. Purple Kush's foliage exhibits a classic indica growth pattern: a sturdy bush with dark green hues and hints of purple toward ripeness.

Purple Kush is versatile, performing well for both indoor and outdoor growers. She does very well in a screen of green (SCROG) setup. Purple Kush buds form tight chunky nuggets with hints of purple in the tips of the calyxes, as well as the tops and underside of the leaves. Finishing in a solid 8-week flowering period, she has a soft pine bouquet and a sweet, grapey taste on an earthy foundation. Her very frosty veneer of glands will please both the connoisseur of indica potency and the hashish fan. The Purple Kush high is strong, sedating, and stretches on for hours. While she is a moderate yielder, Purple Kush's long, deep stone delivers when it comes to treating chronic pains and inflammations, among other conditions.

 I 100% indica

 body relaxation, heavy

 sweet, grape

 50-60 days

 Hindu Kush ♀/
Purple Afghani ♂

 15-30 g/plant in;
1.5 lb./plant out

 SOG

  70I/30S

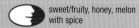 body relaxation, clear-headed

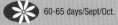 sweet/fruity, honey, melon with spice

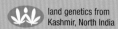 60-65 days/Sept/Oct.

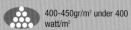 land genetics from Kashmir, North India

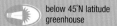 400-450gr/m² under 400 watt/m²

below 45°N latitude greenhouse

 SOG

Sadhu is an homage to the legendary ganja from India's high altitude valleys, and to the wandering ascetics, or *sadhus*, who keep the traditions of cannabis cultivation and ritual and recreational use alive. Sadhu's parentage is a combination of a specially adapted landrace male from the Himalayan heights, and one of Mandala's short flowering indica-sativa hybrids. This strain is a terrific choice for beginners, or anyone who desires a high yielding and potent indica that requires only basic plant care to thrive.

Mandala's latest seed stock has improved the uniformity of the flowering time and height among individual plants without losing any of their hybrid vigor. Sadhu is Mandala's shortest indica, finishing at 2½ to 3½ feet (80-100 cm)—a robust and compact stature ideal for restricted spaces such as grow boxes, or incognito balcony grows, or for raising bushy, medium-tall plants outdoors. Sadhu thrives in all grow systems, including organic systems that use quality potting soil. Her controlled size make her a good sea of green strain. For indoor cultivation in soil, Mandala recommends forcing Sadhu into flowering when the plants reach about 2 feet.

Outdoor cultivation works best up to 45° North latitude or in climates with a dry autumn. This hardy, weather-resistant variety will usually finish by mid-September in Southern latitudes. In extreme Northern climates, expect to wait 2 weeks longer. If clones are planted late, around summer solstice, their flowering time can be shortened by up to two weeks. Excellent results can also be achieved in the greenhouse.

Trichome production is very generous on Sadhu's leaves and buds. These plants develop a fresh sweet candy aroma, with some leaning toward a bubblegum scent (although there is no relation to the strain of that name). As they dry, these beautifully rounded buds take on a sweet-fruity honeydew melon scent and flavor with just a bit of spice in the exhale. Sadhu's resiny leaves and buds produce generous amounts of wonderfully fragrant hash of fine quality that is reminiscent of India's traditional hand-rolled *charas*.

The word *sadhu* originates from Hinduism and describes an ascetic holy man (the women ascetics are called sadhvi). These are the stereotypical wise mountain hermits, living in caves, seeking wisdom, and through their spriritual practices, burning off karma. Mandala's Sadhu strain offers a meditative indica high—relaxed and oceanic, but clear-headed. This potent effect builds up gradually, coarsing through the body in a warm current; it can be overwhelming if smoked continuously before the full effect creeps up on you. Sadhu's peaceful stone can sooth stress-related disorders such as hyperactivity and insomnia. Some medical growers also report that it has antidepressant properties and the strain has benefited cancer patients.

Mandala Seeds
Mike and Jasmin, Mandala Seeds founders, globetrotters and cannabis breeders for several decades

During our world travels, particularly in India and Nepal, we were fortunate to discover and collect seeds from a wide variety of landrace genetics. In the early 1990s we had already recognized the need for innovative and fresh genetics to revive vigor in a market dominated by cross- and inbreeding. Over the following decade we pursued well-defined breeding goals to develop strains that meet all expectations of modern indoor and outdoor growing, while at the same time exhibiting hybrid vigor derived from the ancient power of landrace genetics. The results are strains with fast and strong growth, heat resistance, high yields, "old school" aromas and well-balanced highs that are a trademark of Mandala hybrids.

The Mandala seed bank is based upon guidelines that we believe reflect the spirit of this sacred herb: sharing and caring. We value ethical business practice and the trust growers invest in our seed bank. One of our most important contributions to the cannabis market is to provide quality F1 hybrids. We work to keep costs low and we have strict quality controls on seed selection and germination rates.

Mandala growers has a web forum and web site for feedback from the grower community. Assisting med patients is very important to us and we consider feedback from patients in our breeding. We enjoy sharing our knowledge on cannabis and our strains and we welcome everyone to join in the "mandala" (circle) of cultivators.

Somaui

Soma Seeds

Right photo: Ed Rosenthal

S I 80S/20l

awake, creeper

sweet, tropical

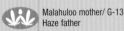
98 days/end Nov.

Malahuloo mother/ G-13
Haze father

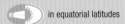
40-60 g/plant

in equatorial latitudes

As the name suggests, this variety derives from genetics taken from one of the cannabis sweet spots of the globe, the Hawaiian Islands. Somaui's mother, Malahuloo, combines with the G-13 Haze for a tropical, sativa-dominant strain. Somaui's sweet and gradual high offers a little beach vacation for sativa fanciers.

Somaui is a wide plant that branches extensively, making it most suitable as a large plant, a good quality for those concerned with plant numbers. As Somaui moves through its growth phases to ripeness, lime green buds form along the long lanky branches, making surprisingly thick white hairs, which gently turn pink as the buds ripen. In the temperate regions, this variety is confined to the indoors, where it takes 14 weeks to finish. Soma prefers to grow Somaui in soil, using organics such as guano, which make for a high quality, flavorful yield. In tropical environments, Somaui finishes at the end of November.

Somaui plants that begin flowering at approximately 2 feet (60 cm) will reach 5 feet (1.5 m) at finish, taking the shape of a willowy spruce. Her delicate, wispy branches form thin sativa-style chartreuse leaves. She is a sensitive type, and will react when faced with adverse conditions or drastic changes in environment. Soma recommends this variety for advanced farmers with connoisseur tastes for sativas.

The joys of Somaui begin in the grow room, where one must resist the temptation of a premature harvest due to the exquisitely sweet aroma that wafts from her buds as they travel toward ripeness. The technical skill and lengthy season required for this variety are rewarded with long, thick, slightly airy buds that are mold-resistant and easy to manicure. Yields are respectable, around 1 1/2 to 2 ounces (40-60 g) per plant.

Somaui is ethereal. Her sweet tropical-flavored high creeps up with an effortless transition and a long effect. The high is very uplifting, clear-minded and awake. At its best, it is nothing short of spiritual. As such, this variety is a guaranteed attitude adjustment, and a potential treatment for depression.

Second Place, *Highlife* Cup, Bio-Sativa category 2006

Soma's garden

Somini

Soma's Sacred Seeds

 60I/40S

 down tempo, sleepy

 Afghani hash

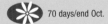 70 days/end Oct.

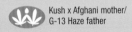 Kush x Afghani mother/ G-13 Haze father

 30 g/plant

in subtropical climates

In the ganja world, the terms "kush" and "haze" promise connoisseur-grade indica and sativa, respectively. Somini brings together a Kush strain from the homelands of the indica varieties, and a sativa-dominant G-13 Haze father, to deliver a compact, nearly even combination of indica and sativa that prospers indoors or out.

Somini stays small, reaching 4 feet at harvest. With her minimal branching and controlled size, this strain is a great choice for sea of green cultivation and for gardeners with limited space. Somini's G-13 Haze genetics extend her flowering phase beyond what is typical of indicas, but at 10 weeks, this is a moderate cycle for haze-influenced varieties. This strain stands up well to adversities and recovers well when exposed to especially hot or cold conditions. Given that haze sativas can be temperamental, this variety is attractive for beginners who want a little haze in an easy-to-grow package.

Outdoors, Somini is appropriate to subtropical climates, where she finishes in late October. Indoors, Soma prefers to grow this strain in soil using primo organic fertilizers such as guano. These plants come with a hearty appetite—they will eat a lot given the chance. Using this method, yields of around 1-2 ounces per plant can be expected.

Somini is a squat, dark green plant that turns purple when exposed to cool temperatures. Her buds are like compact clusters of popcorn; they become adorned with crystals as they ripen. The plants have a spicy green aroma that permeates the air and requires precautionary measures if neighbors are within whiffing distance.

The Somini high is strong and sleepy with a cured aroma and flavor of Afghani hash. It comes on fast, bringing that hooded eyelid look of extended relaxation. Soma and his wife Donamaria started this variety together, and they believe that the result is a good strain for together time. So cozy up under a blanket on the sofa with some snacks, or take a lazy moment to lounge in a patch shady lawn on a summer afternoon. Enjoy a little downtime with some Somini and your honey.

Sour Cream

DNA Genetics

 SI 70S/30I

 calm, sedating

 sour, floral

 70-77 days

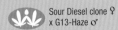 Sour Diesel clone ♀ x G13-Haze ♂

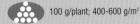 100 g/plant; 400-600 g/m²

 greenhouse

 SOG

Sour Cream descends from two powerful North American lines. The New England "diesels" are non-haze sativas that push marijuana's citrus-like pungency into the realm of fuel. Sour Cream's mother is the near-pure sativa Sour Diesel, a clone-only strain derived from Chem crossed with Mass Super Skunk. This version of Sour Diesel is known for her sour Kush-like smell and her stand-out sour candy taste. The father, G-13 Haze, is a cream of the crop male that shows his true colors in this cross, but with improved yield. Sour Cream brings these two North American strains together for a complex, unusually calming stone.

This sativa-leaning strain is most suited for indoor cultivation, but can also be grown in greenhouses or outdoors. While no particular characteristics of this strain rule out any growing methods, DNA generally grows in soil with organics, preferring to vegetate for 3 or 4 weeks and grow fewer plants to larger sizes. Sour Cream is a picky eater and doesn't like too much warmth. Maintaining a consistent but moderate feeding regimen and a cool temperature range will assure the best results with this strain.

During her vegetative stage, Sour Cream looks like an indica, with fat fan-shaped leaves. She starts to grow upward rapidly as soon as she enters flowering. By the fifth week, her leaves grow out long and slender like a sativa's. In six more weeks, it's harvest time. Sour Cream's buds are slightly fluffy but not as airy as many sativa-dominant plants. This variety produces between 400 and 600 grams per square meter.

Cured and dried Sour Cream buds resemble haze buds, and share the sour taste of the Diesel. But where the classic haze high is energetic, even speedy, Sour Cream offers a tranquil mind vacation. Some users will want nothing more than a few spare hours, a recliner, and a bowl of snacks; others will appreciate a more purposeful calm, and a relief from the mental and physical fatigue of the daily grind.

Sour Diesel IBL

Reservoir Seeds

Thirs strain's heritage draws on North American Dead Tour genetics that bring together New England and the Rockies of Colorado. Reservoir created an IBL, or "inbred line" over three years' time in order to produce a uniform strain from a plant that was only available as a kick-ass clone. The Sour Diesel IBL has been crossed with itself to stabilize the line into a sativa-dominant indoor/greenhouse strain that reeks of lemon and fuel, and a high that can only be described as "unforgettable."

Reservoir's Sour Diesel IBL was specifically bred for the controlled environments of indoors or greenhouse settings. Like all marijuana, it can be grown outdoors given the right climate—in this case, the southern U.S., the tropics, and like latitudes. Indoors, Reservoir's Sour Diesel IBL prefers average feedings with a recommended pH of 6.0 in hydro and soil. This strain is for growers who have their rooms and their skills dialed in. However, as long as the basic rules of thumb for growing marijuana are followed, this strain will move through its cycle looking like picture-perfect weed.

When flowered at one foot (30 cm), Sour Diesel IBL roughly triples in height during flowering phase, forming the characteristic conifer-like profile. This strain is a good candidate for sea of green when properly pruned; FIMming also works well. Otherwise, she should be multi-topped for best results. Her leaves will initially be somewhat thick and squat, thinning as the plant reaches maturity. Average flowering times run around 11 weeks, although hydro grows may ripen sooner. All growers, beginners and experienced alike, can expect average to above-average yields typical of a sativa-dominant strain—up to 1 gram per watt of indoor light.

The Reservoir Sour Diesel's growing cycle may be comfortably normal, but growers will find their results are far from "middle of the road." Ripe buds are tight and photo-worthy, and they reek of diesel and taste of sour lemon candy. The odor is strong enough

 75S/25I

 up, psychedelic

 lemon, fuel

 77 days

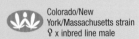 Colorado/New York/Massachusetts strain ♀ x inbred line male

 1g/watt

 tropical latitudes greenhouse

 SOG

to permeate brick walls. Serious odor control is a must for growing this strain, even if you don't have neighbors.

Sour Diesel IBL's high is a soaring, psychedelic, lemon-flavored lift into the sunshine. It levels out in a clear-headed euphoria, good for most activities aside from operating heavy machinery and driving that golf cart too fast. Overindulging can limit activities to the recreational, but moderate toking puts you in a deeply good mood. It is a great stone for letting the negatives go. Many medicinal users find Sour Diesel IBL a good variety for treating sadness and pain.

As "East Coast Sour Diesel," this strain swept the sativa categories at the 2005 *International Cannagraphics'* IC420 awards. Crops from Reservoir's Sour Diesel line won both First and Second place in the Sativa Grower's Cup, while the seeds themselves won Third Place in the Sativa Breeder's Cup. Reservoir's Sour Diesel also won the *High Times* Strain of the Year award in 2005.

Speed Queen

Mandala Seeds

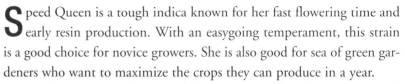

S peed Queen is a tough indica known for her fast flowering time and early resin production. With an easygoing temperament, this strain is a good choice for novice growers. She is also good for sea of green gardeners who want to maximize the crops they can produce in a year.

Speed Queen is resilient in rough outdoor weather, finishing in mid-September in southern latitudes. In cooler climates, expect ripening to take an additional two weeks. For indoor cultivation, the breeder reccomends growing a screen of green, or topping the plants. Given extra vegging time, and adequate pot size, topped Speed Queen plants will grow a forest of enormous colas. Indoor grows reach harvest in a fast 8 weeks. Due to her vigor and thick stems, this strain also delivers quality cuttings over a long period of time as a mother plant.

Speed Queen has resistance to spikes in heat. She forgives the occasional mistake in plant care and grows robustly with good soil with low levels of feeding. This strain is a boon for people with little time or energy for their garden. Harvesting and trimming is a quick operation since all buds grow chunky. The bud leaves and even the sun leaves are covered in frosty trichomes, which are good for hashish. One phenotype has the delicious aroma of orange and citrus. The other mixes fresh fruitiness with a more pungent/skunky note.

The aromas transform to a sweet or fresh-fruity smell and flavor once the buds are cured. Compact, resiny, and pleasant-smelling, her buds have great "bag appeal." For an indica, Speed Queen has a surprisingly stimulating and balanced mind-body high that does not put you to sleep. Mandala refers to this strain as the "surfers' choice." Surfers are true connoisseurs who sample a lot of fine grass at the world's best surfing spots. They like to stay on their feet, on the board or at a party. The "surfers' choice" is a potent, sociable buzz that you can ride like a wave. The high comes on quickly and is pleasantly relaxing, yet leaves plenty of energy for enjoying a full moon party, or just watching the waves roll in.

 mostly indica

 mind/body, relaxing, social

 citrus, skunky

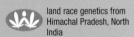 55 days/Sept.

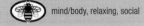 land race genetics from Himachal Pradesh, North India

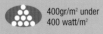 400gr/m² under 400 watt/m²

 SOG

Feminized Seed
Ed Rosenthal

Feminized seeds produce only female plants. When they germinate there will be nary a male among them. The threat of accidentally pollinating crops by missing identification of a male is eliminated. A male-free crop is only one reason why one might produce all-female seeds. Another goal might be the preservation of a particular characteristic or plant type. The predominant way to preserve the exact genetics of a plant is by cloning of one sort or another. However, a plant crossed with itself (called self-crossing) offers a much better chance of retaining favorable characteristics. Another reason for using this technique is to create a hybrid of two female plants. What to do if no male of that variety is available? If a branch of the female can be turned "male," there would be pollen to cross the plant with itself or any other female. By eliminating males from the equation, breeding becomes much easier.

Feminized seeds are produced by inducing a normal female, not a hermaphrodite, to grow male flowers with viable pollen. This pollen is collected and used to produce seed. The sperm in the pollen contains only female or X chromosomes because the plant has no Y, or male chromosomes. Voila! The progeny will inherit an X from the sperm in the pollen and an X from the egg donor. The resulting seeds can only inherit two X chromosomes, which means that all resulting seeds will be girls!

Congratulations!

Feminized seeds are not as mysterious or weird as they might seem. In mature human males, female hormones cause feminizing changes such as breast enlargement, softened body lines, and a higher pitched voice. The primary sex organs have already

Buds often produce male flowers as they reach stage 3 ripeness. Not much pollen is produced, but a little goes a long way.

been formed but they shrink. When the treatment ends, the influence of the feminine hormones ceases and the male characteristics gradually reappear. The same thing happens with plants treated with masculizing chemicals. The difference between effects on higher animals and plants is that mature animals have already formed their sex organs. Every time a plant grows a new flower, it is growing a new sex organ. Flowers under chemical influence grow in a viable masculine form. However, the plant is still a female with two X chromosomes, so the sperm in the pollen only has X sex chromosomes.

There are several methods used to produce feminized seed. By far the easiest method was developed by Soma, the noted breeder. He noticed that when colas reached late ripeness, which by the way, I prefer as the harvest-time, a few viable male flowers appear. This is not only a signal that the buds are ripe. The pollen from these flowers can be harvested using a fresh watercolor brush and a small glass or metal container. Not all varieties produce male flowers at the end of ripeness, but many do, and they do it reliably.

Plant stresses often induce hermaphroditism in cannabis. However, I haven't found stress techniques reliable. These only seem to work when you don't want them to. Irregular light cycles and heat stress sometimes induce male flowers but I haven't found a stress regimen that insures masculinization. Should this happen accidentally in a garden with a valuable variety, be opportunistic. Collect the pollen, even if you have no plans to use it. It remains useable for years when packed with a desiccant and stored in a sealed container in a freezer.

A spike of male flowers. The five-petaled flowers turn upward as they open. The pollen produced by the anthers is light and borne on the wind or falls to the leaves below, as seen here.

Some varieties flower normally outdoors. However, when clones of the same plant are grown indoors the plants undergo stress and grow hermaphrodite flowers. The pollen from these male flowers can be used for breeding, provided that the resulting plants are going to be grown outdoors, where they won't exhibit the unwanted hermaphroditism.

These plants are stretched from their treatment with gibberellic acid

The use of chemicals is the method used in laboratories and in commercial production to induce male flowers in female plants. Two chemicals that are used are gibberellic acid and silver thiosulfate. Both of these chemicals inhibit the plant's ethylene production, a hormone that promotes female flowering. As a result, the plant's female flower production is reduced. However, these chemicals also have a second mode of action because other ethylene inhibitors don't promote male flowering. The actions are localized. If only one branch of a plant is sprayed, that branch will be the only one affected. The rest of the plant will continue growing female flowers, not males.

Gibberellins are hormones that plants produce to regulate many phases of their growth. Several of the gibberellins, GA3, 4, 5 and 7, induce male flowers on female plants when they are sprayed before the plants initiate flowering. GA3, which is the gibberellin most commonly available commercially, is the most effec-

Close-up of a branch treated with gibberellic acid.

tive. A solution of 0.01% (0.1 gram GA3 in a liter of distilled water) is best. Lower doses result in fewer male flowers. Higher amounts have an inhibitory effect. Lightly spray the tops of the plant for five consecutive days and then place the plants in flowering regimen by increasing the uninterrupted dark period to 12 hours a day. The sprayed area will stretch a bit, but within two weeks the first signs of male flowers will appear. They will be ripe and ready to release pollen in another two weeks.

Silver nitrate can also be used to induce male flowers. A solution of 0.02-0.03% is sprayed on the plant and then the plant is placed in the flowering regimen of 12 hours light, 12 hours of uninterrupted darkness. The leaves will droop for a day or so and then resume turgidity. Male flower growth will become apparent in a couple of weeks. They will ripen a few weeks later. To make a 0.02% solution, add 0.1 gram of silver nitrate in 0.5 liters of distilled water.

Silver thiosulfate is more effective than silver nitrate; that is, it will induce more male flowers. It is made by combining two water solutions, one containing silver nitrate and the other, sodium thiosulfate. The exact formula is below. The plant is sprayed until the liquid drips off the leaves and immediately after, the light regimen is changed from vegetative to flowering. The sprayed areas yellow a bit and stop growing for a few days. Then they start to grow male flowers, which ripen in a few weeks.

Male and female flowers on a hermaphrodite that resulted from being treated with gibberellic acid.

The Formula:

Mix 0.1 gram silver nitrate in 100 ml (3.5 ounces) distilled water. Stir rapidly until dissolved (Solution A).
Mix 0.5 gram sodium thiosulfate in 100 ml distilled water. Stir rapidly until dissolved (Solution B).
Pour Solution A into Solution B.
Dilute Solution A/B 1:9 with distilled water. That is, add the solution to a 2-liter container. Fill to top with distilled water. The solution is now ready to spray.

Spoetnik #1 ♀♀

Paradise Seeds

Photos: Trichome Pharm

Spoetnik #1 is a versatile plant with excellent resistance to a wide variety of horticultural problems. She is compact, and offers an unusually cerebral stone for a pure indica—an uplifting, meditative awareness without the snooze afterwards.

Indoors, Spoetnik #1 adapts well to all types of growing styles, with slightly higher yields in hydro or coco mediums. Paradise recommends using fertilizers with ample amounts of calcium, magnesium and iron during the flowering stage. When placed into flowering at one-foot heights, these plants finish at just over 2 feet tall.

Paradise named this variety after the first spacecraft ever in orbit. Spoetnik #1 has a spectacular growth cycle, the breeder explains: "Although she has a short flowering cycle, 7 to 8 weeks, her slow start may cause growers concerns. Is she stressed, or going to take much longer than suggested, or maybe she's just not going to yield much? Then—voila! Suddenly, out of nowhere, she bursts forth around day 38 or 40 of the flowering cycle. She shoots up and out in size so quickly, you could almost see her growing if you sat and observed for a few hours. Perhaps more exciting, the flowers that were looking rather petite begin to proliferate with lovely calyxes. Like her namesake rocket, Spoetnik #1 seems to be revving her engines, storing up everything she is fed for the countdown in the last 2 weeks of flowering, when she explodes with amazing power." By harvest, the plants look oily, thanks to their heavy coating of glands. Her colas form into rockets: long and cylindrical.

Gardeners can expect to see two phenotypes. One phenotype exhibits pinkish hues in its resin and pistils and also has a refreshing strawberries-and-cream smell. The other phenotype is more purple-hued. She tastes like dark Corinthian grapes mixed with a mineral, astringent touch on the exhale. Her high is much more meditative and focused. The purple phenotype proves a bit more difficult to grow than the pink phenotype.

 100% indica

 cerebral, clear

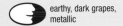 earthy, dark grapes, metallic

 50-55 days

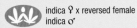 indica ♀ x reversed female indica ♂

 500 g/m² under 600 watts/m²

 SOG

152

The effects of this pure indica strain are surprisingly uplifting, with no physical crash at the end. The high is felt mostly on the top of the head and in the face, excellent for working days when you want to get stoned but not overdo it. Anecdotal reports from the Canadian medicinal marijuana community suggest that Spoetnik #1 is a good strain for multiple sclerosis patients.

Sputnik

TGA Seeds

 70S/30I

 body stone, sleepy, uplifting and trippy

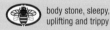 berry, spicy pepper

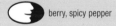 56-63 days/mid-Sept.

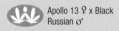 Apollo 13 ♀ x Black Russian ♂

 5 oz./ plant

Subcool calls this strain Sputnik because it crosses his space-themed Apollo 13 strain with a Russian. The original Sputnik I satellite ushered in the Space Age when the Soviet union launched this basketball-sized satellite into a quick orbit around the earth in 1957. The Black Russian strain used in Sputnik is a Blackberry (Somablaze) x AK-47 (Nebu) cross that comes from a gene pool in which every female turned solid purple. Like a combined Russian-American space mission with both astronauts and cosmonauts, Sputnik offers two phenotypes, similar in growing characteristics, but very different on the inside, in taste and stone.

Both Sputnik phenotypes perform well in indoor and outdoor gardens, with impressive yields. Sputnik germinates very easily. She starts slow in the vegetative phase, due to her Blackberry influence, but grows fast once established; plants budded at 30 inches (almost 1 meter) reach final heights just over 4 feet (120 cm). Subcool reccomends topping these plants in the classic candelabra shape, and binding them to expose her lower branches to the light. "Bush" and "screen of green" are the two best growing profiles for Sputnik. She does well in hydro systems with plant supports. Cabinet growers will love the way this plant maximizes yields by branching out to fill small areas. Sputnik's leaves are very wide, with deep serrations; they start off dark green and tend to fade to a lime as the plant matures.

Sputnik dislikes direct heat, and does very well in a peripheral bud room location. Outdoors, she may not yield to potential in cold climates. Her slow recovery from stress means that you will need some patience to clone her. This variety finishes in mid-September outdoors in Northern California, or after just 8-9 weeks indoors.

The most common Sputnik phenotype favors her Black Russian father, with red-spectrum coloration and an indica stone. This pheno starts changing color around week five, and shifts from light pink to vivid magenta by harvest. The purple pheno's buds are big, fluffy, and resinous, almost eggplant-colored, with a slightly spicy palate. Her stone is a deep, long-lasting body relaxer that comes on fast.

The other phenotype leans toward the white and green spectrum, and the blasting sativa high of Apollo 13. This pheno is much more fragrant—a cream soda smell, with some sour undertones as she ripens. Her buds are denser and more nugget-like than the purple pheno's. Her stone is a fast involuntary smile, a euphoric flight that can leave veteran stoners blissed out and staring at the walls. Trippy visual effects, like seeing real trees in cartoon vision, are common. The high is similar to the marvelous Apollo 13, but with a sweeter taste and a slightly more psychedelic quality.

Both phenotypes give the user a strong stone with a kiss of well-being behind it. Subcool recommends writing, thinking, talking, music and art as good activities while in Sputnik orbit. Appearing in public might be less easy, as you may be more inclined to let your goofy side out to play.

(Arjan's) Strawberry Haze ♀♀

Green House Seed Company

Photos: Jan Otsen

 70S/30I

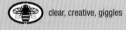 clear, creative, giggles

 strawberry

 75 days/mid-Oct.

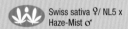 Swiss sativa ♀/ NL5 x Haze-Mist ♂

 500-600g/m² in; 800g/plant out

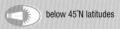 below 45°N latitudes

A rjan's Strawberry Haze is a bright green mid-sized sweet sativa. She descends from Swiss stock on her mother's side, and popular Northern Lights and Mist varieties on the paternal side. These seeds are feminized, meaning that they will all grow out as bud-producing female plants. The Strawberry Haze's buds have the aroma of an almost candy-like strawberry, and her smoke is sweet-tasting with an upbeat high.

This mountain plant is adapted to humid areas, and overall very versatile, strong, and easy to grow. She ranges from 3 feet in small containers, to 10 feet when her roots are given free reign. She has short internodes and medium-sized round leaves. Her branches tend to shoot out vertically, straight toward the light, allowing plants to be placed closer together than is possible with more rangy sativas. Three to four plants per square meter is an ideal arrangement.

Strawberry Haze performs best and delivers the utmost in strawberry flavor when grown in soil. Hydro systems can be used to increase the yield, but the taste is less sweet. Green House recommends a light hand when it comes to nutrients, as this plant is more sensitive to overfeeding than most sativas. Start with a low pH (5.6 hydro / 5.8 soil) and slowly increase to reach 6.5 at the end of flowering. Extra P and K should be added after the 5th week of flowering. The maximum EC should be 1.9 in hydro and 1.7 in soil. Flush plants at the end of flowering, which takes about 10-11 weeks or until mid-October outside.

Arjan's Strawberry Haze finishes with chubby buds, composed of rounded calyxes that are thickly coated with resin and thin long hairs. Aside from the expected, very sweet strawberry aroma, which is much sweeter than most sativas, the smell has also been compared to summer blossoms, rose petals and red berries. Her high is fast hitting, clear, creative and giggly. It is good for social moments as well as for introspective ones. Chasing the blues away, making love, making friends laugh, and making art are all recommended activities to accompany this strain. Arjan's Strawberry Haze was created by Arjan in the period 2000-2004. He introduced it on the market in 2006, after winning the 1st prize among Green House's strains at their Very Important Smokers Panel event in 2005.

Sweet 105

Greenthumb Seeds

awake, body stone

spicy, hashy sandalwood

105 days from seed to finish

Endless Sky ♀ x secret ♂

2-4 oz./plant

greenhouse

The most invisible pot harvest is the one that's already gone when the police show up on their autumn sweeps. In Dr. Greenthumb's Sweet 105, stealth is maximized with a short, feminized indica that auto-flowers and takes 105 days from seed to harvest. The yield and potency had to be strong before this unique strain met Greenthumb's criteria. The result is a plant that ranges in height from 1-3 feet at finish, with excellent potency, and a harvest date well before September.

Greenthumb Seeds specializes in outdoor strains that grow well in temperate environments. For Sweet 105, Dr. Greenthumb crossed a secret father with his well-loved Endless Sky, a popular indoor/outdoor Iranian strain adapted to outdoor growth in Canada that has been a potent, high-yielding staple for sea of green growers for years.

In outdoor grows, Sweet 105 can be planted directly in the ground any time after the last spring frost, or started in a cold frame or greenhouse, or under lights indoors to be set outside when danger of frost has passed. For maximum outdoor yields, Sweet 105 should be started the last week of February or first week of March, so peak flowering occurs during the longest days of the year in early to mid-June. On this timetable, harvest will come in late June or early July. Gardens can be started later, or planned so that multiple crops can be grown from spring to fall, so long as they're timed to finish before the first "killing" frost.

Sweet 105 is bred for outdoor cultivation. If you choose to grow her inside, take advantage of her auto-flowering characteristic by increasing the photoperiod throughout the flowering cycle to 14-18 hours of light instead of the classic 12/12, which will maximize growth. Sweet 105's minimal branching and single-cola dominant growth pattern can also work to the advantage of the indoor grower. Yields per plant average at 2-4 ounces (55-110 g). There is some phenotype variation among the plants. One phenotype (about 2 plants out of 15) takes an extra 3 weeks to finish, but with yields doubled to 8 ounces. Growers may also find a couple (about 2 in 15) "ankle-biters" in the bunch, that stay dwarfed and finish fast, in 90-100 days, but only weigh in at about an ounce when harvested. In many cases, cuttings can be taken and rooted when a vegetative and rooting photoperiod of 24 hours of light is employed.

Sweet 105 buds are compact, silvery-colored cones with a fast onset and a high that endures for hours. The buzz is strong, more "stoned" than "high," but the effect is awake, with a nice sandalwood/incense flavor more typical of hashish. This strain will also make copious amounts of hash if so desired.

The Church ♀♀

Green House Seed Company

Photos: Jan Otsen

The L.A.-based heavy metal band, System of a Down, sat in with Green House breeders on a little variety naming session back in 2005 when they appeared on the Very Important Smokers panel. They helped Green House to arrive at the name "The Church" after the lyrics in one of their songs.

This mostly indica variety is suitable in temperate and mountainous environments as well as balmy regions more conducive to outdoor grows. She is particularly well suited for areas with high levels of humidity due to her extraordinary mold resistance. Indoors, this plant performs best in soil-based gardens, although she also does well in hydroponic systems. The Church is a rugged, adaptable plant that branches moderately to form a rounded bush of modest height. Her mid-sized internodes are more extended than most indicas. Green House recommends spacing these plants at one per 2 square feet to allow each one to fulfill her potential. Pruning might also be in order to direct the plant's energy into her most valuable branches.

The Church can soak nutrients, especially in hydro setups. The pH should be started at 5.6/5.8 and slowly increased to 6.5 at the end of flowering. The maximum EC should be 2.1 in hydro and 1.8 in soil. Plants require 9 weeks to ripen and should be flushed in the last weeks to ensure the best quality and flavor.

This plant flushes to purple rather quickly if exposed to low night temperatures. Her mature buds are replete with thick short hairs. The Church's round clustered nuggets of bud take on a sage-like sheen due to the silver-gray tone of the resin.

The predominant sensation on first smoking The Church is mental stimulation and ease, followed by a steady descent into the body, which feels clean and loose-limbed for many hours afterwards. Tastewise, spring flowers and red berries keep the flavor light and sweet. Rather than the jolt of heavy-hitting strains, The Church offers a mild, progressive high that doesn't rule out work, play or socializing.

 70I/30S

 mind/body

 floral, berry

 63 days

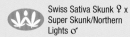 Swiss Sativa Skunk ♀ x Super Skunk/Northern Lights ♂

 700-800 g/m² in; 900g/plant out

The Doctor ♀♀

Green House Seed Company

Photos: Jan Otsen

Valentino Rossi may be one of the greatest motorcycle racers of all time. Now in his late 20s, he has come to dominate the sport in a decade of riding, claiming seven World Champion titles in the Grand Prix racing circuit. Although he's been known by a few nicknames, "Rossifumi" and "Valentinik" among them, most people simply call him "The Doctor." As you may have guessed, this Green House strain is named in tribute to Rossi. Like her motorcycle-racing namesake, The Doctor's stone blasts on the scene, hitting quick and hard, reverberating through the head and body with an intensity that might encourage couchlock. This is zero-to-one-hundred fast accelerating indica.

A champion producer, this mostly indica variety generates the heaviest, most dense bud of Green House Seed's collection. Besides being a powerhouse of production and stone, The Doctor is also an easy-to-grow plant that performs well for beginners and experienced growers alike. Soil-based setups will deliver sweeter tastes, but hydro delivers a bigger yield. Outdoors, this variety matures properly in temperate and Mediterranean zones as well as in subtropical regions, finishing around the end of September in the Northern hemisphere.

The Doctor is a bushy, indica-dominant plant that requires trimming to clear away her lower branches, and prefers 2 square feet of space per plant. This variety enjoys generous feedings, especially in hydroponics systems. Green House recommends adding extra phosphorus and potassium about midway through flowering, in week 4, in order to maximize flower development. EC levels should not exceed 2.4 in hydro and 2.0 in soil.

The buds on this plant may remind you of primitive totems peeping out of a jungle. Massive colas jut out from the fat dark green leaves, looking oddly out of proportion to the short bushy stature of the plant. Rounded calyxes shoot in all directions from the cola profile. The flavor is sweet, earthy indica with a skunky background.

 80I/20S

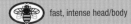 fast, intense head/body

 pungent sweet

 56 days

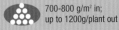 Great White Shark x South Indian ♀ x Super Skunk ♂

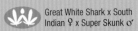 700-800 g/m² in; up to 1200g/plant out

The Purps

BC Bud Depot

Photos: Purps #1 & BC Bud Depot

This scrumptious purple plant comes out of Mendocino County, in northern California, where she began as a clone-only plant among the medical marijuana community. BC Bud Depot has developed a stable cross to make Purps seeds available. The Purps is a good in indoor and outdoor environments, finishing well in a coastal British Columbia climate.

The Purps is a pungent girl with medium thick leaves and green hues that turn more purple as the plant ripens. Her moderate side branching makes her amenable to both pruning for a sea of green garden, and, alternatively, encouraging her to spread out as a multi-branch plant. BC Bud Depot prefers growing The Purps in soil with medium organic feedings, because it enhances the flavors in this smooth and complex strain—hints of buttery caramel coffee and woodsy floral pine.

Indoors, The Purps reaches an average 3-4 feet (around 1 m) at harvest, while outdoors she can grow to 6 or 8 feet (2-2.6 m). Her height can be controlled by shortening the vegetative phase, which may also influence her final crop. The Purps's indoor yields range from 1.5 to 2.5 ounces (40-70g) per plant, while outdoor plants will produce 4-5 ounces (120-150 g) each. These plants require 8-9 weeks to finish, which places harvest in the last half of October. Although she is a hardy, pest-resistant strain, the Purps is more suited for gardeners with a few crops under their belts.

The buds are tasty looking and smelling, with deep purple coloring and a frosting of resin. The flavors are soothing and tantalizing, lingering pleasurably on the tongue. The Purps high soars into a longlasting purple haze of playful euphoria. It produces an active, awake feeling with a very low burnout factor. A nice antidote to depression, these rich flavored buds turn the blues to the Purps.

 60S/40I

 giggly, blissful

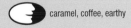 caramel, coffee, earthy

 56-63 days/late Oct.

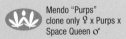 Mendo "Purps" clone only ♀ x Purps x Space Queen ♂

 50-100 g/plant in; 750 g/plant out

 SOG

The Third Dimension

TGA Seeds

Photos: Subcool

In this sativa-dominant variety, breeder Subcool brings together three elite strains from the TGA Library. The super potent Apollo-13 mother, a Subcool personal favorite, is combined with a pick of the litter male Jack the Ripper, itself a combination of the primo Jacks Cleaner and Space Queen strains. Considering the strength of these three strains, TGA feels that this hybrid is a new dimension in three-way crosses.

The Third Dimension is a fast finisher indoors, reaching ripeness in just under 8 weeks. The plant shown here was grown in an organic super soil mix. This variety has nice lateral branching and thrives when topped and allowed multiple heads. Expect a classic morphology from this strain —an evergreen profile with stems as strong as the parent branches. She is a light eater, taking moderate feedings and growing well without supports.

The Third Dimension plants express two phenotypes, one that is more indica and one that is more sativa. The short indica phenotype is well suited for SCROG (screen of green), because her side branching makes a nice lower bud shelf. She shows minimal stretching and finishes very fast, in just over 7 weeks. This plant is worth cloning and has shown good success at rooting. The less common sativa-dominant phenotype takes an additional two weeks to finish, and springs up to over 5 feet tall, but her soaring high is worth the extra wait. The phenotypical variation in this strain makes her desirable to growers who love both indicas and sativas.

As Third Dimension matures, her resin spreads even to fan leaves, causing the small "sugar" leaves to curl together. Bubble hash made from these leaves melts completely at the touch of a flame. The plants' green hues change into autumnal shades as harvest approaches. The buds are chunky and hard, with a sharp pointy shape. Cured buds are light green with brilliant orange hairs and a sticky coat of resin.

The Third Dimension fills the grow room with the dank smell of sour, overripe fruit.

 70S/30I

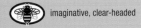 imaginative, clear-headed

 tropical, fruit

 52-70 days

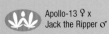 Apollo-13 ♀ x Jack the Ripper ♂

As the buds dry, the aromas and flavors mellow to a tropical fruit tartness. The inhale has an infusion of fruitiness that includes hints of mango, pineapple, coconut and a bit of lemon. The exhale is very soft and mellow. When smaller leaves are converted to bubble hash, it completely melts when heat is applied.

Third Dimension's buzz is a sparkle added to the mundane day, making everything softer and funnier. In moderation, this stone is clearheaded enough for daytime enjoyment; however, this is the weed equivalent of a tropical cocktail—the light fruity flavors can make you forget the potency, so it sometimes too easy to overindulge. The Third Dimension may enhance snacking, but is likely to rev up the imagination a bit too much to encourage sleep.

T.N.R.

KC Brains

Outdoor growers in temperate or wet climates should consider a test-drive of T.N.R. This outdoor-only strain pairs an early, moderate indica from KC's seed collection, the KC-2, with a Thai sativa that has grown outdoors in Holland for over three decades. The resulting strain a hybrid with an indica background and strong Thai-style sativa tendencies.

Grown outdoors in soil, T.N.R. forms long internodes and extended branching, transforming into a giant Christmas tree that creates its own ornaments—terrific hooked colas that remain bright green behind a proliferation of red stigmas and white crystals. This variety prefers commercial fertilizers over organics. She has been bred to finish successfully in the cloudy, cool weather of her adopted home, and has great mold resistance. T.N.R. takes 10-12 weeks to ripen in Holland, with harvests around mid-October. This strain also performs well in drier and sunnier southern climates, such as Spain, where she finishes a few weeks earlier.

T.N.R. is fairly conspicuous when allowed to grow unchecked. She shoots up quickly during the vegetative phase, and can reach heights of 12 feet (3.5 m). At that size she looks more like a tree than a plant, with a sturdy trunk of a main stem supporting branches, shaggy with cones of bud and long slender, tropical green foliage. At finish, T.N.R. plants can easily yield a kilogram (2.2 lbs) each; in very sunny areas, expect even more.

The buds are classic Thai weed, and are even suitable for stitching into Thai sticks. Even though T.N.R. is only slightly sativa-dominant in parentage, the Thai genes come through forcefully in her high—a strong creative-intellectual awakening with an electric, almost psychedelic edge. This kind of uplifting high is a good cure for the blues. T.N.R. is also great for an afternoon of shooting the breeze with friends, socializing and thinking up ideas. Seasoned pot connoisseurs who miss Thai will be pleased with T.N.R.'s aroma and flavor: sweet, but rounded with hints of cinnamon, clove and black pepper. It's likely to make old Thai fans sentimental, and make newer tokers into Thai fans.

 60S/40I

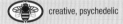 creative, psychedelic

 sandalwood, floral

 70-84 days

 adapted Thai ♀ x KC-2 indica ♂

 1+ kg (2.2 lbs.)

 SOG

True Blue

DJ Short

When the breeder of the original Blueberry releases a variety named "True Blue," Blueberry fans are in for a delight. DJ Short's True Blue was carefully selected from a double Blueberry cross. The Blueberry variety originally derives from a marriage between a female with Thai and Oaxacan roots, and an Afghani indica male. The strain's characteristic lavender tones were inherited through the mother's genetic line.

DJ Short's flavor connoisseurship influences his growing preference for soil-based gardens with organic nutrients, but his varieties adapt well to hydroponics, aquaponics or aeroponics systems. True Blue has a light appetite for nutrients, especially nitrogen, although these plants will be happy with generous helpings of worm castings and bat guano.

Like her Blueberry parents, True Blue forms many branches, especially when topped, and finishes at a medium height. Beginning a lusty dark green, these plants develop the soft lavenders for which they were named, as well as a mouthwatering sweet musky odor. Some plants show variegated (crinkled) leaves that are a benign inheritance from the Thai family. This hybrid's flowers have petite calyxes that form along tight spade-shaped buds, taking on a "fox-tail" structure.

True Blue finishes in 8-9 weeks on average indoors. Outdoors, she ripens in late September to late October depending on latitude. In a location near the 45 degree North latitude, she was successfully harvested within the normal growing season. True Blue's finished buds have photo-worthy color, and their aroma mellows from its musky quality to a fruity floral sachet once cured.

The True Blue buzz is a lucid, inspiring, social high that creeps up gradually. This is pot to share! Friends will admire the connoisseur flavors, and the warm euphoria of True Blue's stone will make for a fun and congenial smoke-out.

 50S/50I

 social, creeper, euphoric

 blueberry

 55-65 days/late Sep. to late Oct.

 Blueberry ♀ x Blueberry ♂

 25-50g/ft.² at 50w/ft.² or 1 g/w

(Arjan's) Ultra Haze #1

Green House Seed Company

Photo: Jan Otsen

Arjan's Ultra Haze #1 is a mighty sativa, the deep green daughter of a Neville's Haze/Cambodian mother and Laotian father. This strain rewards the grower with a very strong high. It all but kicks you into a new level of mental awareness and visual pleasure. The effect is lucid, stimulating and ethereal, good for inner exploration activities such as meditation, yoga, dance, painting or singing. The flavor is pungent, a mixture of menthol, musk and pine, followed by a strong incense aftertaste with notes of earth and sandalwood.

Ideally, a crop of this strain should be organized with one plant for every square meter (10 square feet). Arjan's Ultra Haze #1 follows her haze heritage, growing into a large, lanky weed that may reach heights of over 12 feet when planted with no root limitations. To keep the size around 5-6 feet, plants should be cultivated in 2-gallon size containers. Although branchy, this sativa doesn't get in her own way—her limbs form at 45-degree angles to the main stem, allowing light to reach the inner part of the plants and ripen the flowers in a uniform manner. Her pliable branches have long internodes where substantial colas will form, creating a need for support as the crop approaches harvest. By then, her branches will droop under the weight of the buds, which are unusually compact, dense, and resinous for a sativa, with long, thick hairs and a very irregular shape due to her wild calyx development.

Indoors, Arjan's Ultra Haze #1 can be grown in hydro or soil. As is typical, hydroponics tends to maximize indoor yields at the expense of intensity in flavor. This variety has a good resistance to pests and to heat, but it fears cold nights. She likes normal quantities of feedings, with some extra P and K in the last four weeks of flowering. Outdoors, this near-pure sativa must be raised in a climate with a long growing season, as she will not finish until the end of November in the Northern Hemisphere. South of the equator, Arjan's Ultra Haze #1 will finish by mid-June.

 90S/10I

 clear, introspective, meditative

 menthol, musk, pine, earthy, sandalwood incense aftertaste

 84-91 days/late Nov.

 Neville's Haze x Cambodian sativa ♀ x Laos ♂

 900g per/m² in; 1300g/plant out

171

(Arjan's) Ultra Haze #2

Green House Seed Company

Photo: Jan Otsen

Like Arjan's Ultra Haze #1, Arjan's Ultra Haze #2 stems from a Laotian father and a Neville's Haze mother, but this variety's mother is also half Mango Haze. The result is a medium-sized haze sativa with medium-short internodes, a luscious taste and a shorter flowering time than its cousin. Although she finishes about a week earlier, Arjan's Ultra Haze #2 still requires an outdoor location that can allow for an 11-12 week flowering period. Indoors, this strain is suitable for either hydroponics or soil-based systems.

Unrestricted, these plants reach 10 feet (300 cm) heights, but when limited to small containers, they finish at 5-6 feet (150-180 cm). The branches of Arjan's Ultra Haze #2 shoot out at a 30-degree angle, but her structure is very uniform and balanced, allowing light to reach the inner flowers. Even though her overall height and branch formations are shorter than many haze-heavy varieties, and her branches are sturdier, Arjan's Ultra Haze #2 may still require support in late flowering. Plants should be spaced at one per square meter (3 square feet) for optimum results. Extra phosphorus and potassium are recommended after the 7th week of flowering, with added flushing in the final weeks to avoid salt accumulation. Arjan's Ultra Haze #2 has good resistance to pests.

This variety's buds tend to close up after 6 or 7 weeks of flowering, making cone-shaped colas that are impressively dense and compact for a sativa. Long thick hairs poke out from the flowers, and the entire bud acquires a grayish glaze of resin that offsets its intensely dark green. Arjan's Ultra Haze #2's leaves are large and stereotypically sativa, with elongated leaflets.

Green House's tests of this strain revealed THC levels at over 20%, so it is not surprising that Arjan's Ultra Haze #2 gives a very strong, fast and almost trippy high, with a well balanced body vibration. Within the spectrum of haze highs, this one is on the fun,

  S I   90S/10I

 strong, fun, mind/body balanced

 mango and incense

 77-84 days in, Nov. out

 Neville's Haze x Mango Haze ♀ x Laos ♂

 700-800g/m² in; 1000g/plant out

in equatorial regions

giggly side as it evens out. Absurdities and punchlines are everywhere when you smoke this strain, especially with like-minded friends. It is a terrific variety to enhance a bubbly or chatty mood for sparky social situations. Arjan's

Ultra Haze #2 has a very fruity sativa flavor, reminiscent of freshly cut mango, with undertones of sandalwood and celery.

What Are Trichomes?

Prepared by Pistils

With thanks to contributions from Red Eyed Farmer and Snaps Provolone for the majority of the text and diagrams.

Cannabis resin glands are called "trichomes" These little lovelies begin to develop as soon as the plant starts growing, but the real explosion of trichomes comes during flowering.

Head on view of trichomes.

Why Did Ttrichomes Evolve in Nature?

Trichomes protect the plant, flower and especially the developing seeds from insects, animals, environmental conditions and diseases. The cannabinoids and various components of essential oils lend their protective qualities to these glands.

Insect Protection: Many insects find the thick sticky coating of trichomes unpleasant. Others get caught in the sticky trichomes. Some of the cannabis oils have repellent qualities to various herbivores. This offers a layer of protection from infestation by certain insects. It is especially useful for guarding the developing seeds.

Animals: The THC and other oils that make up the contents of trichomes have psychotropic effects that many mammals and other herbivores find unpleasant. This makes cannabis less palatable to many herbivores & omnivores. Fewer snackers means more chance of survival and reproduction.

Desiccation: Trichomes help to 'insulate' the pistilate (female) flower from low humidity levels and high wind.

UV-B Light: UV-B light is a form of ultraviolet light that can be harmful to living things, THC has very high UV-B adsorption properties and more THC is produced in high UV-B light conditions. This implies that THC provides the plant with some protection from this harmful light.

Fungal and Bacterial Protection: Some of the oil components present in trichomes inhibit the growth of fungi and bacteria.

→ capitate stalked glands → capitate sessile glands
→ bulbous trichomes → cystolith hairs

Trichome Structures

While structurally diverse, trichomes tend to come in three basic variants.

Bulbous: The *bulbous* type is the smallest (15-30 micron) trichome style. One to four cells make up the "foot" and "stalk," and one to four cells make up the "head" of the gland. Head cells secrete a resin—cannabinoids and various terpenes which accumulate inside the balloon-like head cells. When the gland matures, a nipple-like protrusion may form on the membrane from the pressure of the accumulating resin. The bulbous glands are found scattered about the surfaces of the above-ground plant parts.

→ capitate stalked glands → capitate sessile glands
→ bulbous trichomes → cystolith hairs

Capitate-Sessile: The second type of gland is much larger and more numerous than the bulbous glands. These trichomes are called "capitate," which means having a globular-shaped head. On immature plants, the heads lie flush, appearing not to have a stalk. For this reason they are technically called "capitate-sessile." They actually have a stalk but it is only one cell high, so it is scarcely visible beneath the globular head. The head is usually composed of eight cells, but can be up to sixteen cells, and forms a convex rosette. These cells secrete cannabinoids and terpenes, which accumulate between the rosette and its outer membrane. This gives it a spherical shape. The gland measures from 25 to 100 micron across.

Capitate-Stalked: During flowering, the capitate glands that appear on the newly formed plant parts take on a third form. The "capitate stalked" gland consists of a tier of secretory disc cells which is topped by a large secretory cavity. Some of the glands are raised to a height of 150 to 500 micron when their stalks elongate.

Cannabinoids are found in greatest abundance in the "capitate-stalked" gland. These capitate-stalked glands form their densest cover on the female flower bracts during flowering. They are also highly concentrated on the small leaves that accompany the flowers. The male flowers have stalked glands on the sepals, but they are smaller and less concentrated than on the female bracts. Male flowers form a row of very large capitate glands along the opposite sides of the stamen.

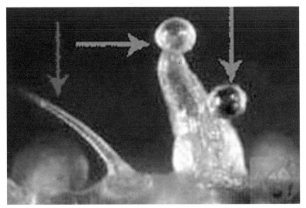

Magnification of glands along surface of leaf. Red-cystolith hair; green-capitate stalked gland heads, one of which has been decapitated.

Copious numbers of trichomes grow along leaf edge.

Life inside a capitate-stalked trichome

diagram by Red Eyed Farmer

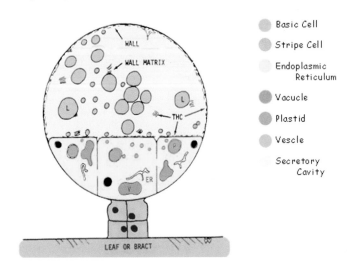

- Basic Cell
- Stripe Cell
- Endoplasmic Reticulum
- Vacucle
- Plastid
- Vescle
- Secretory Cavity

When to Harvest your Trichomes

There are several schools of thought as to the best time to harvest. I shall attempt to explain how you can determine the harvesting time that will produce the most favorable psychoactive effect for your individual preferences.

We are most concerned with the capitate-stalked trichomes, as these contain the overwhelming majority of the psychoactive cannabinoids, of which Delta-9 THC is the star.

Heavy trichome production is not necessarily an indication of a potent plant. Some hemp strains have moderate layers of trichomes yet only deliver a strong headache. In a recreational or medicinal marijuana strain, a thick layer of trichomes is the first indication that it may well possess an elevated potency level, but it is certainly not a guarantee. It is also necessary that those glistening glands are filled with potent THC.

A small 25x or stronger pocket microscope, which can be picked up inexpensively at an electronics store like Radio Shack or Maplins, works well for getting a closer peek at your trichome development. The goal is to examine the capitate-stalked glandular trichomes for the coloration of the gland heads, which varies between strains and with maturity. Most strains start with clear or slightly amber heads which gradually become cloudy or opaque when THC levels have peaked and are beginning to degrade. Regardless of the initial color of the secretory cavity, with careful observation you should be able to see a *change in coloration* as the bud ripens.

Red arrows indicate glands that remain clear, while yellow arrows show trichomes that have become cloudy and opaque.

The diagram above denotes clear trichomes with red arrows, the yellow arrows mark cloudy trichomes, and the green arrows mark the amber trichomes.

Some cultivators wait for about half of the secretory cavities to turn opaque before harvesting, to ensure maximum THC levels in the finished product. Of course nothing tells the truth more than your own perception, so try samples at various stages to see what is best for you and the *phenotype* you are growing. While you may be increasing the total THC level in the bud by allowing half of the glands to go opaque, the bud will also have a larger percentage of THC breakdown products such as CBN, which is why some people choose to harvest earlier while most of the secretory cavities are still clear.

Indica varieties will usually have a 10-15 day harvest window to work with. Sativas and Indica/Sativa hybrids often have an extended period to work with.

THE CANNABINOIDS

THC:
Delta-9-tetrahydrocannabinol & delta-8-tetrahydrocannabinol—THC mimics the action of anandamide, a neurotransmitter naturally produced in the body, which binds with the cannabinoid receptors in the brain to produce the "high" associated with marijuana.

THCV:
Tetrahydrocannabivarin—prevalent in certain South African and Southeast Asian strains of cannabis. Although THCV may possess many of the therapeutic properties of THC, it does not contribute significantly to marijuana's potency.

CBD:
Cannabidiol—previously believed to be psychoactive, or to contribute to the high by interacting with other cannabinoids. The most recent research indicates that CBD has a negligible effect on the high. It is however a strong anti-inflammatory, and may take the edge off some THC effects, such as anxiety. Although a non-psychoactive cannabinoid, CBD appears to be helpful for many medical conditions.

CBN:
Cannabinol—a degradation product of THC, CBN is not psychoactive, but is believed to produce a depressant effect or "fuzzy" forehead when it is present in significant quantities.

CBC:
Cannabichromene—this cannabinoid is a non-psychoactive precursor to THC.

CBG:
Cannabigerol—a non-psychoactive cannabinoid. Hemp strains often possess elevated levels of CBG while possessing only trace amounts of THC.

Photo: Ed Rosenthal

Venus

Nirvana

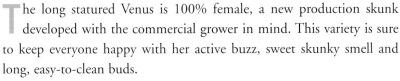

The long statured Venus is 100% female, a new production skunk developed with the commercial grower in mind. This variety is sure to keep everyone happy with her active buzz, sweet skunky smell and long, easy-to-clean buds.

Venus is a combination of a consistent, stable Pure Power Plant and a strong Top 44 female that was forced to produce male flowers using giberellic acid. The Pure Power Plant (PPP) is one of the most well known and widely available commercial strains in Europe. Developed in the late 1990s from South African and Dutch strains, PPP proved to have terrific flowering potential in the indoor garden scene and has become a staple of Dutch growers. Coffeehouse patrons appreciate PPP's upbeat buzz and light pine-tree scent.

Top 44 is another wildly successful commercial plant that displays minimal branching, a pungent skunkiness, and a satisfyingly rapid grow cycle. Her easy-to-control growth has made Top 44 desirable for indoor or balcony growers, and a natural choice for sea of green setups.

The result of this union is an ideal indoor 50/50 hybrid that yields dew-dusted buds after 8-10 weeks of flowering. Venus grows well outdoors in Spain and Great Britain, where she finishes in October. In indoor grows, modest heights of 3 feet (1 m) can be expected when flowering is induced at 1 foot (30 cm).

While Venus naturally takes on the traditional candelabra structure, Nirvana recommends pruning away her spindly bottom branches and retaining her top five limbs, staking them in a sea of green style, with 16 plants per square meter. Indoors, hyrdoponics systems will deliver the best volume and a more dense carpet of glands. Venus can handle a very high EC and therefore should be pushed to achieve her full potential. The cured Venus buds have a curious aroma that is decidedly skunkish, and an agreeable level of potency that reaches both body and mind in a soothing yet wakeful way—a kind and balanced stone.

 50S/50I

 cerebral, soothing

 sweet, skunky

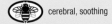 56-70 days

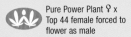 Pure Power Plant ♀ x Top 44 female forced to flower as male

 450-550 g per m² in SOG

 SOG

Very Berry Haze

Apothecary

 100% sativa

 energetic, relaxed

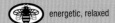 boysenberry pie

 70-80 days

 East Coast ♀ and ♂

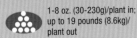 1-8 oz. (30-230g)/plant in; up to 19 pounds (8.6kg)/ plant out

 greenhouse

This Haze plant is a U.S. native, coming from East Coast genetics that were passed along to the medical marijuana breeders at Apothecary. It is a pure sativa, and as such is best grown as an indoor or greenhouse plant, outside of the equatorial zones.

Very Berry Hazes exhibit all of the stereotypical qualities of the haze-dominant sativas. They grow rapidly into jumbo plants, shooting out a profuse number of long flexible branches with many bud sites. Because of their tendencies, they are really only suitable as multi-branch plants. They should be started in flowering quickly in order to keep heights reasonable. Indoor plants that are forced at 6-inch (15 cm) heights can finish about 10 weeks later at 4 feet (120 cm). They can finish outdoors by the first of November in appropriate regions of California, growing to 12 feet (4 m) when started at 8 inches (20 cm). Very Berry's foliage is a lush green with thin leaflets, and may be prone to developing mold if attempted in colder climates, or if the indoor room is kept at brisk temperatures. These plants are most suitable for soil-based gardens.

Very Berry buds begin as little popcorn-ball formations that elongate to create large buds by harvest. In a sunny outdoor environment, Very Berry Haze can yield prodigiously, reaching harvests up to 19 pounds. Indoor yields per plant depend on gardening style, and can range between 1-8 ounces per plant.

The Very Berry Haze acquired her name for her delicious flavor, which Apothecary compares to the more obscure boysenberry. This berry, named after its breeder Rudolph Boysen, combines the raspberry, blackberry and loganberry, for a fruit that is more pungent and earthy than its relatives. Fans of the berry will begin to smell the edge of fruit as these plants reach maturity, and will find a jammy-sweet, robust boysenberry taste to the finished product. The high is the soaring, awake and mentally refreshing influence of the haze sativa. It's a bliss-out for beach or mountain solitudes, or something to be shared with a sweetheart when you want to just kick back together and reflect with gratitude on the mysteries of being alive.

Wappa

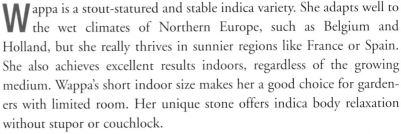

Paradise Seeds

 100% indica

 energtic

 pungent fruit, marshmallows

 55-60 days

 indicas

 400-500 g/m² in; 400-500/plant out

 SOG

Wappa is a stout-statured and stable indica variety. She adapts well to the wet climates of Northern Europe, such as Belgium and Holland, but she really thrives in sunnier regions like France or Spain. She also achieves excellent results indoors, regardless of the growing medium. Wappa's short indoor size makes her a good choice for gardeners with limited room. Her unique stone offers indica body relaxation without stupor or couchlock.

Wappa is a feminized variety: pollen was obtained from a female manipulated to produce male flowers, so all of Wappa's seeds will produce females. She is a robust plant that quickly becomes the darling of the grow room because of her attractive appearance, ease in cultivation and fast ripening and yield. Her broad leaves shine with lime-green healthiness. She starts a bit slowly, but soon gets her pace, turning into a picture-perfect little spruce with one main stem. When forced to flower at 1 foot (30 cm), she doubles in size by maturity, producing big chunky colas that fill the air with sweet aromas of fruits and sugar. Wappa has a high calyx-to-leaf ratio, which makes her a breeze to manicure. She finishes flowering in about 8 weeks, by which time her buds and the neighboring leaves will be coated in resin that smells like marshmallows. This variety produces about half a kilogram (about 1 pound) of buds per square meter indoors, or roughly the same amount per plant, outdoors.

Wappa's fruity nugs are great head candy. Her THC has been measured at over 18% on all samples, making for an intense high. The buzz comes on strong, but with a pleasant rather than jarring onset. It is a luminous high that nudges open the doors of perception. After a few hours, the heightened awareness fades off slowly, leaving an appreciation for the mini-vacation that Wappa has created. Even though she is a full indica, Wappa does not weigh down the body or create couchlock for most people. She taps into an active, aware body vibe, more conducive to merrymaking than couch surfing.

White Berry ♀♀

Paradise Seeds

Photo: DrBreiTor

 75I/25S

 happy, lucid

 berry, lemon

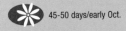 45-50 days/early Oct.

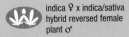 indica ♀ x indica/sativa hybrid reversed female plant ♂

 400-500 g/m²

 SOG

White Berry is a happy-go-lucky plant that is very fast to flower and particularly well suited to sea of green grows. Because her seeds have been feminized, White Berry plants are all-female, with no sexing required. When this variety was tested, none of her seeds showed hermaphrodite tendencies—there was not a single male flower formation among these ladies.

White Berry is model marijuana, slender and medium in height, with fresh green good looks and a single-cola dominance and homogeneity between the plants that will endear her to sea of green gardeners. These plants come up in a uniform pattern that makes growing and budding as easy as growing from clones. The White Berry calyx-to-leaf ratio is good news for weed manicurists, because she is easy to trim. Her smaller leaves are also worth recycling for excellent hashish.

In her short 7-week flowering phase, White Berry becomes bejeweled with trichomes that frost her buds, and she generates a decidedly berry perfume that leaves no doubt about the appropiateness of her name. Some calyxes may turn purple, giving them an exotic and mouthwatering appearance. Although the buds will look as if they are on the verge of ripeness at 6 weeks, it is best to leave them another 10 days to allow the cannabinoids to reach their peak. By then, the ripened buds will add a fresh astringent lemon to the unmistakable berry scent, like a mixture of berry jam and citrus. The flowers will have bulked out, achieving yields in the 400-500 grams per square meter range.

White Berry's hybridized genetics create a complex and versatile smoke. The typical result is a crystalline sativa head high, complementary to most lightweight activities. Yet when smoked in higher quantities, an indica-style body stone comes forward, like a warmth radiating over the smoker's torso and limbs. Tokers who smoke lightly throughout the day, but want a deeper stone at night, may find that White Berry meets all their needs in one attractive, easy-growing package.

White Rhino

Green House Seed Company

Photo: Jan Otsen

White Rhino is a strong, fast-growing, near-pure indica with ancestry in the same lineage as her more famous relative, White Widow. As the name suggests, this plant is tough and sturdy, with a thick skin for high temperatures as well as cold nights. This strain delivers a knockout, medicinal-grade indica stone.

White Rhino adapts well to any environment, and is known for her massive yields, especially in hydro grows. Green House recommends starting her with a medium-low pH (5.7 hydro, 5.8 soil) that is slowly increased until it reaches 6.5 at the end of flowering. EC levels should be kept under 2.4 in hydro and 2.0 in soil. Plants ripen in 9 weeks, or early October. To really see the rhino's "white," let her ripen one extra week.

While these plants flourish in SOG or SCROG systems, they can also be grown in larger containers and allowed to vegetate into bushes. The White Rhino plant has a typical short squat stature, with short, thick branches and extremely compact internodes. She is a smart choice for indoor gardeners with space limitations, or outdoor growers looking for a shorter plant. Plants grown in 5-gallon containers will finish at 4-5 feet (1.2-1.5m) if allowed to grow vegetatively for at least two weeks. With less veg time, or in small containers, plants stay at about 3 feet (1 m) tall. Even plants with no root limitations finish no taller than 6 feet (2m). When White Rhino is allowed to grow big, pruning is necessary to allow light and air to penetrate the inner and lower areas of the plant.

The leaves on White Rhino are huge, full, and midnight green, and her stalks are very thick. Her calyxes are small, round and super dense, forming rock hard colas. While not terribly odiferous while growing, the White Rhino harvest will have a pleasantly sweet smell. The toke is also sweetened with indica berry flavor, followed by a sharp aftertaste and sometimes a bout of coughing. White Rhino delivers a full-throttle indica stone. The buzz goes straight to the body, giving a rubbery, relaxed feeling that is nearly narcotic. It

 90I/10S

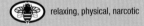 relaxing, physical, narcotic

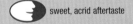 sweet, acrid aftertaste

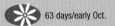 63 days/early Oct.

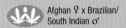 Afghan ♀ x Brazilian/ South Indian ♂

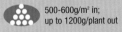 500-600g/m² in; up to 1200g/plant out

 SOG

is a down-tempo smoke that endures, ideal for slow-paced recreation. White Rhino is prized in the medical community for effective relief of chronic pain.

2nd Prize, *High Times* Cannabis Cup 1996, Bio category
2nd Prize Champions Cup, Madrid 2005

White Satin

Mandala Seeds

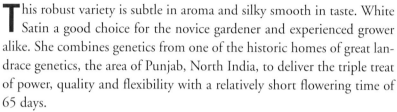

This robust variety is subtle in aroma and silky smooth in taste. White Satin a good choice for the novice gardener and experienced grower alike. She combines genetics from one of the historic homes of great landrace genetics, the area of Punjab, North India, to deliver the triple treat of power, quality and flexibility with a relatively short flowering time of 65 days.

White Satin has a slim growth pattern, with medium-long side shoots and a generous main bud that is perfect for sea of green from seed or clone. This 50/50 hybrid is also versatile enough to make a good SCROG or multi-branch plant. White Satin's main flower power is located on her central stem, but her side shoots also deliver quality "nuggets."

The stems are firm and can easily support heavy colas in outdoor locations. Even under low light, such as under fluorescent tubes, White Satin's performance is very satisfying; however, for optimal yields, Mandala recommends 400 watts or more per square meter. White Satin also performs well when grown in soil with organic nutrients. This strain's medium height, good yield and well-balanced, intensive high have made her a popular variety for all levels of indoor cultivators. Plants can be started and harvested with fairly minimal effort.

Because White Satin can develop an extremely large and dense main cola, during the last 2 weeks of flowering it's a good idea to keep humidity under 50%, and temperature above 68°F (20°C) in the dark cycle, as a preventative measure against mold. Outdoors, she does best up to 48 degrees latitude or in climates with a dry autumn.

White Satin's buds are characterized by a broad oval shape and large calyxes. The most resinous plants will cover many leaves with trichomes and provide an extra treat for hash enthusiasts. White Satin's growing odor is light—and stealthy—but pleasant. The cured buds exude a mild apricot aroma and a fresh sweet taste. This is a pleasure smoke, with a fresh, mentally stimulating high, but no heavy body or mind incapacitation. That makes her a great, functional choice for a daytime enjoyment.

 50S/50I

 clear, uplifting

 mellow apricot

 65 days

 landrace genetics from Punjab, North India

 400-500g/m² under 400w/m²

 SOG

White Smurf

Ceres Seeds

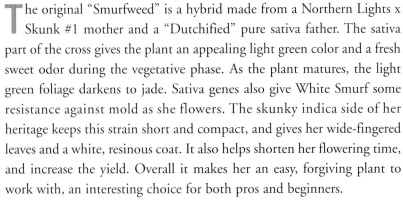

 50S/50I

 body warming

 citrus and musk

 45-55 days in/Oct. out

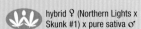 hybrid ♀ (Northern Lights x Skunk #1) x pure sativa ♂

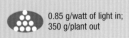 0.85 g/watt of light in; 350 g/plant out

 greenhouse

The original "Smurfweed" is a hybrid made from a Northern Lights x Skunk #1 mother and a "Dutchified" pure sativa father. The sativa part of the cross gives the plant an appealing light green color and a fresh sweet odor during the vegetative phase. As the plant matures, the light green foliage darkens to jade. Sativa genes also give White Smurf some resistance against mold as she flowers. The skunky indica side of her heritage keeps this strain short and compact, and gives her wide-fingered leaves and a white, resinous coat. It also helps shorten her flowering time, and increase the yield. Overall it makes her an easy, forgiving plant to work with, an interesting choice for both pros and beginners.

White Smurf can be grown indoors, in a greenhouse, or outdoors depending on the climate. Indoors, White Smurf grows to medium height, with a solid bud and not many side-branches. With a little pruning at the start of flowering, White Smurf is very suitable for the sea of green method. This plant develops beautiful solid, sticky, snow-dusted colas. Little towers of calyxes sprout on her buds when she flowers. As the buds become covered with crystals, the flowers themselves remain green and white with orange accents in their hairs, a trait marking the skunk side of the hybrid.

Reflecting her skunk and sativa heritage, White Smurf's flavor has been described as "full and rich," "musky-but-sweet" and "powerful," but it has also been described as "fresh" and "citrus-like." Her stone is both relaxing and wakeful. After one joint, this strain gives a deep, warm body-buzz that feels like walking through water, but doesn't stupefy or lead to snores. White Smurf starts a smooth reggae rhythm pulsing though your body, a social, happy, positive vibe that makes a superb after-dinner smoke. Cannabis Cup attendees agreed – they showed their appreciation by awarding this strain with the People's Choice as well as the overall Cup in 2000.

Wonder Woman

Nirvana Seed Bank

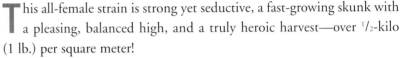

This all-female strain is strong yet seductive, a fast-growing skunk with a pleasing, balanced high, and a truly heroic harvest—over $^1/_2$-kilo (1 lb.) per square meter!

Wonder Woman's mother is ICE, an award-winning strain (1998 Cannabis Cup) that combines Afghani, Skunk, Northern Lights and Shiva genetics into a very stable plant with a rich layer of trichomes, a heavy stone and a fuel-like aroma. This mother was winner in the 1998 Cannabis Cup. Her "father" is actually another female plant, a beautiful Top 44 that Nirvana manipulated using giberellic acid to produce male flowers. Top 44 is one of Nirvana's flagship commercial strains. It's the fastest-flowering indoor variety they have, ripe and ready in just over 6 weeks under perfect conditions. As a smoke, Top 44 is deep and skunky with a long lasting buzz. These parents give Wonder Woman her superpowers—fast maturation, mighty yields, feminized seeds (there are no males in the bunch), and a durable high. This amazing amazon lassos the stoner for a long, relaxing stay on Paradise Island, a land of bliss and contentment in body and mind.

Wonder Woman is inconspicuous and does not branch too much, making her ideal for confined gardens such as balconies, or for sea of green farming. This 60/40 hybrid is quite indica in appearance, reaching only $2^1/_2$ feet (80 cm) when flowering is induced at $1^1/_2$ feet (50 cm). Outdoor plants usually reach a petite 4-5 feet (1.5 m) at full maturity.

For the best THC levels, indoor cultivation is recommended. Nirvana prefers hydroponics for the strongest yields and the most solid colas. One especially good technique for Wonder Woman is to prune her top plus four branches, staking them in a sea of green setup with 16 plants per square meter. That can translate to a superheroic yield of 700 grams per square meter under 600 watts of light. This plant can also be pushed to high EC levels—2.4 to 2.6. Outdoors, Wonder Woman produces mega-buds in Mediterranean climates like Spain or California, but her powers are weakened by mold susceptibility in humid areas. Wonder Woman's buds are very dense, and easy to trim.

 60I/40S

 mind/body high

 skunky

 49-63 days

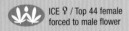 ICE ♀ / Top 44 female forced to male flower

 700 g/m² in SOG

 SOG

A-Train • Afropips First Grade Malawi Go
Arjans Haze #1 • Arjans Haze #2 • A
BC Blueberry • BC God Bud • BC Swee
Blue Buddha • Blue Cheese • Brainstor
Chrystal • Cinderella 99 x Panama Red •
First Lady • Fruit of the Gods • Fruity Tha
Grape Ape • Grape Krush • Hashberry
Jack the Ripper • Jacky White • Jilly
Kiwiskunk • Kushage • LA Confidential •
Green • Motavation • Mothers Finest •
Purple Kush • Sadhu • Somaui • Somini
Queen • Spoetnik #1 • Sputnik • (Arjar
Church • The Doctor • The Purps • T
(Arjans) Ultra Haze #1 • (Arjans) Ultra
Wappa • White Berry • White Smurf • Wh

d • AK-48 • American Dream • Arctic Sun
ans Haze #3 • Aurora Borealis • B-52
Tooth • Big Bang • Big Buddha Cheese
n Haze • Burmese Kush • Casey Jones
D-Line • Ed Rosenthal Super Bud • F-13
• G-13 Diesel • Gonzo #1 • Grandaddy
Hash Heaven • Haze Mist • Ice Cream
ean • Kaya • KC-36 • KC-45 • Kish
owryder #2 • Mako Haze • Martian Mean
Mount Cook • Nuken • Opium • Posh
Sour Cream • (IBL) Sour Diesel • Speed
) Strawberry Haze • Sweet 105 • The
e Third Dimension • TNR • True Blue
Haze #2 • Venus • Very Berry Haze
e Rhino • White Satin • Wonder Woman

Company Acknowledgments

Afropips

Afropips First Grade Malawi Gold

Represented by:
Gypsy Nirvana's Seed Boutique
www.seedboutique.com, www.seedbay.com
orders@seedboutique.com
Unit 415, Reaver House, 12 East Street
Epsom, Surrey KT17 1HX United Kingdom
tel. (Seed Boutique—Amsterdam shop)
+31 (0)20 638-0404

Apothecary Seeds

Granddaddy Grape Ape
Very Berry Haze

www.apothecarytravel.com
apothecarytravel@yahoo.com
P.O. Box 251
Calpella, CA 95418
tel: 877-687-6461

BC Bud Depot

BC God Bud
BC Sweet God
BC Sweet Tooth
BC Blueberry
Blue Buddha
The Purps

www.bcbuddepot.com

bcbuddepot@hushmail.com
Willemsstraat 20 HS
1015 JD Amsterdam, Netherlands

Big Buddha Seeds

Big Buddha Cheese
Blue Cheese

bigbuddhatalks@hotmail.com
P.O. Box 12822
Birmingham B32 9BB
United Kingdom

Cash Crop Ken

Kish
Nuken
Posh

www.vancouverseedbank.ca

Ceres Seeds

Fruity Thai
White Smurf

www.ceresseeds.com
info@ceresseeds.com
mail: PO Box 10213
1001 EE Amsterdam, Netherlands
shop: Nieuwezijds Voorburgwal 80
1012 SE Amsterdam, Netherlands
tel: +31 (0)20 528-5556

Coffeeshop SR-71

Purple Kush (clones available)

www.OaksterdamNews.com
oaksterdamnews@gmail.com
377 17th St
Oakland, CA 94612
Info: 510-836-NEWS(6397)

Delta-9 Labs

Brainstorm Haze
Fruit of the Gods (F.O.G.)

www.delta9labs.com
info@delta9labs.com
Postbus 14886
1001 IJ Amsterdam, Netherlands
tel: +31 (0)65 234-4921
tel: +31 (0)62 658-2966

DJ Short's Delta-9 Collection

F-13
Grape Krush
True Blue

www.greatcanadianseeds.com
www.legendsseeds.com

DNA Genetics

D-Line
L.A. Confidential
Martian Mean Green
Sour Cream

www.dnagenetics.net
dnagenetics420@hotmail.com
dna@dnagenetics.net
www.myspace.com/dna_genetics
shop address: Sint Nicolaasstraat 41
1012 NJ Amsterdam, Netherlands
tel: (shop 12:00 – 6:00 pm) +31 (0)20 778-7220
fax: +31 (0)20 771-8366

The Flying Dutchmen

Arctic Sun
Aurora Borealis
Haze Mist

www.flyingdutchmen.com
questions@flyingdutchmen.com
O.Z. Achterburgwal 131
1012 DE Amsterdam, Netherlands
tel: +31 (0)20 428-4112

Green House Seed Co.

Arjan's Haze #1
Arjan's Haze #2
Arjan's Haze #3
Big Bang
(Arjan's) Strawberry Haze
The Church
The Doctor
(Arjan's) Ultra Haze #1
(Arjan's) Ultra Haze #2
White Rhino

www.greenhouseseeds.nl
www.kingofcannabis.com
contact through http://www.greenhouseseeds.nl
O.Z. Voorburgwal 191
1012 EW Amsterdam, Netherlands
tel./fax: +31 (0)20 427-3059
Note: no shipment of seeds to U.S.A.

Greenthumb Seeds

Sweet 105

www.drgreenthumb.com
Box 37085
Ottawa, Ontario
Canada K1V 0W9
tel: 613-330-2404

Gypsy Nirvana's Seed Boutique

Afropips First Grade Malawi Gold (Afropips)
Casey Jones (Head Seeds)
Cinderella 99 x Panama Red (Wally Duck)
G13-Diesel (Head Seeds)
Gonzo #1 (Reservoir Seeds)
Sour Diesel (Reservoir Seeds)

www.seedboutique.com, www.seedbay.com
orders@seedboutique.com
Unit 415, Reaver House, 12 East Street
Epsom, Surrey KT17 1HX
United Kingdom
tel: +31 (0)20 638-0404

Head Seeds

Casey Jones
G-13 Diesel

Represented by:
Gypsy Nirvana's Seed Boutique
www.seedboutique.com
www.seedbay.com
orders@seedboutique.com
Unit 415, Reaver House, 12 East Street
Epsom, Surrey KT17 1HX
United Kingdom
tel: +31 (0)20 638-0404

High Bred Seeds
Lowryder #2

www.highbred.net
info@highbred.net
Box 70802, CP Chabanel
Montreal, Quebec
Canada H2N 2L2

KC Brains
KC-36
KC-45
T.N.R.

www.kcbrains.com
P.O. Box 637
4200 AP Gorinchem, Netherlands
tel: +31 (0)65 473-0608
fax: +31 (0)18 363-6510

Kiwiseeds
Kiwiskunk
Mako Haze
Mt. Cook

www.kiwiseeds.com
info@kiwiseeds.com
Prins Hendrikkade 10-11
1012 TK Amsterdam, Netherlands

Magus Genetics
Motavation

www.magusgenetics.com
info@magusgenetics.com
Postbus 36
1600 AA Enkhuizen, Netherlands
tel: +31 (0)22 832-3441
fax: +31 (0)22 832-3467

Mandala Seeds
Hashberry
Sadhu
Speed Queen
White Satin

www.mandalaseeds.com
info@mandalaseeds.com

Nirvana Seed Bank
AK-48
B-52
Chrystal
Kaya
Venus
Wonder Woman

www.nirvana.nl
info@nirvana.nl
St. Antoniebreesstraat 14
1011 HB Amsterdam, Netherlands

tel: +31 (0)20 671-5113
fax: +31 (0)20 671-1361

Paradise Seeds

Ice Cream
Jacky White
Opium
Spoetnik #1
Wappa
White Berry

www.paradise-seeds.com
info@paradise-seeds.com
Postbox 377
1000 AJ Amsterdam, Netherlands
tel: +31 (0)20 679-5422

Reservoir Seeds

Gonzo #1
Sour Diesel

Represented by:
Gypsy Nirvana's Seed Boutique
www.seedboutique.com, www.seedbay.com
orders@seedboutique.com
Unit 415, Reaver House, 12 East Street
Epsom, Surrey KT17 1HX
United Kingdom
tel: +31 (0)20 638-0404

Sensi Seed Bank

American Dream
Ed Rosenthal Super Bud
First Lady
Mother's Finest

www.sensiseeds.com
info@sensiseeds.com
P.O. Box 10952
1001 EZ Amsterdam, Netherlands
Shop: Oudezijds Achterburgwal 150
1012 DV Amsterdam, Netherlands
tel: +31 (0)20 626-2988

Soma Seeds

Hash Heaven
Somaui

www.somaseeds.nl
soma@somaseeds.nl
PO Box 16491
Amsterdam, Netherlands
tel : +31 (0)20 774-6542

Soma's Sacred Seeds

Somini

www.somaseeds.nl
soma@somaseeds.nl
PO Box 16491
Amsterdam, Netherlands
tel: +31 (0)20 774-6542

TGA Seeds

Jack the Ripper
Jilly Bean
Sputnik
The Third Dimension

www.cannaseur.com
subcool@gmail.com
TGA Grow Forums: www.breedbay.co.uk
12-14 Vivian Rd.
Harborne, Birmingham
United Kingdom
tel: +44 (0)121 426-4400

TH Seeds

A-Train
Burmese Kush
Kushage

www.thseeds.com
info@thseeds.com
Nieuwendijk 13
1012 LZ Amsterdam, Netherlands
tel: +31 (0)21 421-1762
fax: +31 (0)20 421-0991

Wally Duck

Cinderella 99 x Panama Red

Represented by:
Gypsy Nirvana's Seed Boutique
www.seedboutique.com, www.seedbay.com

orders@seedboutique.com
Unit 415, Reaver House, 12 East Street
Epsom, Surrey KT17 1HX
United Kingdom
tel: +31 (0)20 638-0404

apical tip: the growing tip of the plant

aeroponics: growing plants by misting roots suspended in air

backcrossing: crossing of an offspring with one of the parents to reinforce a trait

bract: small reduced leaflet in *Cannabis* that appears below a pair of calyxes

calyx: pod harboring the female ovule and two pistils, seed pod

CBC: cannabichromene—one of several non-psychoactive cannabinoids.

CBD: cannabidiol—one of several non-psychoactive cannabinoids; it is anti-inflammatory

F1 generation: first filial generation, the offspring of two parent (P1) plants

F2 generation: second filial generation, the offspring of two F1 plants

feminized: a seed that will produce only 100% female plants.

hydroponics: growing plants in nutrient solution without soil

indica: plant originating at the 30th parallel typified by wide, dark green or purple vegetation; it grows short internodes with profuse branching that form a wide pyramid or assymetrical shape, usually no more than 6 feet tall

internodes: the space between nodes

node: a section of the stem where leaves and side shoots arise; nodes are often swollen, and are sometimes referred to as joints

P1: first parental generation, the parents crossed to form F1 or F1 hybrid offspring

pistils (stigmas): small pair of fuzzy white hairs extending from top of calyx, designed to capture pollen floating in the air

pollen: the male reproductive product that fertilizes the female flower, a a cream-colored or yellow dust released by the male flower which floats along air currents to reach the female

psychoactive: affecting the consciousness or psyche

ruderalis: plant originating from the 50-55th parallel in Russia, typified by the auto flowering of the plant based on age instead of lighting schemes

sativa: plant originating from the 45-50th parallel typified by a tall pine-tree-like growth habit(5 to 15 feet), long internodes, light green color and airy buds

screen of green (SCROG): A technique for supporting plants. A net is secured to a frame and held horizontally so the branches grow through the holes. The net holds the branches in place so they don't bend or droop and helps support them when they are heavily laden with buds.

sea of green (SOG): indoor method for growing marijuana in which many plants are grown close together with little time spent in vegetative growth; rather than a few plants growing large and filling the canopy, many smaller plants are forced into flowering creating a lower canopy and earlier harvest

sepal: a modified leaf located at the base of a flower

stipule: the section where the plant stem meets the leaf stem, or petiole

strain: a line of offspring derived from common ancestors

THC: tetrahydrocannabinol, primary psychoactive component of cannabis

terpene: class of chemicals composed of repeating units of isoprene (C_5H_8) to form chains or 3D structures; associated with various scents and may be responsible for the varied highs in cannabis.

trichome: plant hair that is either glandular (secreting) in function or eglandular (non secreting)

wpf: watts per square foot

wpm: watts per square meter

When Will Your Outdoor Plants Mature?

Cannabis flowers based on the number of hours of uninterrupted dark period it receives. When a critical period is reached for several days the plant changes its growth from vegetative to flowering. During the spring and summer the number of hours of darkness shrinks as the latitude increases. For instance, on June 16, close to June 22, the longest day of the year and the first day of summer, there are 9:30 hours of darkness at the 35th latitude, near Memphis, Albuquerque and Los Angeles. At the 40th parallel, close to New York, Columbus and Denver the dark period is 9 hours. A difference of half an hour. However, the seed producer's latitudes are consider-

Amsterdam Flame strain outdoors Photo credit: Paradise Seeds

ably different than the latitudes of the gardens of many outdoor growers. Vancouver, at the 50th parallel and Holland at the 52nd parallel have 7:49 and 7:27 of darkness respectively on that date. As a result maturity dates change significantly with changes in latitude.

To find the ripening date at your latitude:

1. Count back from the outdoor ripening date the number of days the variety takes to flower indoors.

This is the trigger date, the date that the plant changes from vegetative to flowering phase.

2. Locate the breeder's latitude at the trigger date. The chart (next page) indicates the number of hours of darkness that triggered the plant to flower.

3. On the column representing your latitude, locate the date on the chart that matches the dark period from #2.

4. Count forward the number of days it takes to ripen indoors. The result is the maturity date.

Figuring Ripening Dates: Examples

A variety from Holland ripens there on October 15 and matures in 70 days indoors. Counting back on the latitude chart you see that on August 1, about 75 days before ripening, the plant triggered on 8½ hours of darkness. Along the 40th parallel or further south, the dark period never gets below 9 hours of darkness. The variety will be triggered to flower almost as soon as it is placed outside. If it's planted outdoors June 1 it will ripen in 70 days, near August 10. If planted June 16 it will ripen in late August. At the 45th parallel, the plant will be triggered to flower around July 1. The buds will mature September 10-15.

A Canadian variety adapted to the 50th parallel ripens October 16 outdoors, 60 days after forcing indoors. Counting back to Aug 16, 60 days before the bud matures, the dark period at the 50th parallel is about 9½ hours. At the 45th parallel this dark period occurs August 4, with a ripening date of around October 4. At the 40th parallel it occurs around July 30, with a harvest around September 30. At the 35th parallel and lower latitudes, flowering is triggered as soon as the plants are planted since there are only a few days around June 22 when the dark period stretches longer than 9½ hours. If planted June 1, the plants will ripen in early August.

NUMBER OF HOURS OF DARKNESS BY LATITUDE

Latitude	0	+10	+20	+30	+35	+40	+45	+50	+52	+54	+56	+58
June 16	11:53	11:18	10:40	9:56	9:30	8:59	8:24	7:49	7:27	6:53	6:25	5:53
July 1	11:53	11:18	10:41	9:57	9:31	9:01	8:26	7:41	7:21	6:57	6:29	5:55
July 16	11:53	11:21	10:46	10:08	9:44	9:17	8:45	8:05	7:47	7:25	7:01	7:33
Aug. 1	11:53	11:27	10:59	10:26	10:06	9:44	9:19	8:48	8:32	8:15	7:57	7:35
Aug. 16	11:53	11:34	11:13	10:48	10:33	10:17	9:58	9:35	9:27	9:12	9:59	9:43
Sept. 1	11:53	11:42	11:29	11:15	11:06	10:57	10:45	10:29	10.25	10:18	10:10	10:02
Sept. 16	11:53	11:50	11:46	11:41	11:39	11:35	11:31	11:27	11:24	11:22	11:21	11:16
Oct. 1	11:53	11:59	12:03	12:08	12:11	12:14	12:18	12:22	12:24	12:26	12:28	12:30
Oct. 16	11:53	12:07	12:19	12:35	12:43	12:53	13:06	13:17	13:23	13:30	13:36	13:45
Nov. 1	11:53	12:13	12:36	13:01	13:15	13:31	13:49	14:14	14:24	14:35	14:48	15:03
Nov. 16	11:53	12:21	12:50	13:22	13:42	14:03	14:29	15:00	15:14	15:30	15:49	16:09
Dec. 1	11:53	12:26	13:00	13:39	14:03	14:27	14:58	15:36	16:07	16:14	16:36	17:02
Dec. 16	11:53	12:27	13:05	13:56	14:12	14:40	15:12	15:54	16:13	16:36	17:01	17:31

Seed Producers Latitude Chart:

Australia, Nimbin: Latitude 30° S

Canada: Ottawa-Toronto, Ontario: Latitude 43° N

            Vancouver (incl. Nanaimo), British Columbia: Latitude 50° N

Netherlands: Latitude 52° N

Northern California, USA: Latitudes 36-40° N

Malawi: Latitudes 10-15° S

Spain: Latitudes 39-41° N

United Kingdom: Latitudes 50-55° N

METRIC CONVERSION

Mass

1 gram = 0.035 ounces (1/28 ounce)

1 ounce = 28.35 grams

1 pound = 16 ounces

1 kilogram = 2.2 pounds

1 pound = 0.45 kilograms

Length

1 foot = 30.5 centimeters (1/3 meter)

1 meter =3.28 feet

1 meter = 100 centimeters

1 inch = 2.54 centimeters

Area

1 square meter = 10.76 square feet

1 square foot = .09 square meters

Yield

1 ounce per square foot = 305 g per square meter

100 grams per square meter = 0.33 oz. per square foot

Temperature

15°C = 59°F

20°C = 68°F

25°C = 72°F

28°C = 82°F

30°c = 86°F

32°C = 89.5°F

35°C = 95° F

To figure:

Celsius = (F - 32) x 5/9

Fahrenheit = C x 9/5 + 32

Index

Arctic Sun
Big Buddha Cheese
Casey Jones
F-13
Jack the Ripper
Jacky White
Kushage
Mako Haze
Martian Mean Green
Mother's Finest
Somaui
Sour Cream
Sour Diesel IBL
Sputnik
Strawberry Haze
T.N.R.
The Purps
Third Dimension

 S Sativa Strains (90 to 100%)

Cinderella 99x Panama Red
D-Line (aka Chocolope)
Haze Mist
Malawi Gold
Ultra Haze #1
Ultra Haze #2
Very Berry Haze

 S I Sativa/Indica Hybrids (% unknown)

B-52
Brainstorm Haze (mostly sativa)
Fruit of the Gods (mostly sativa)
Hashberry (mostly Indica)
Kish (mostly Indica)
Nuken (mostly Indica)
Speed Queen (mostly indica)

 S R Sativa/Ruderalis Hybrids

KC-45

 I R Indica/Ruderalis Hybrids

Lowryder #2 (mostly Indica)
Sweet 105 (mostly Indica)

Varieties by Environment

 Indoor Strains

A-Train
Casey Jones
D-Line (aka Chocolope)
G-13 Diesel
Hash Heaven
Third Dimension

 Outdoor Strains

Mako Haze
T.N.R

Indoor/Outdoor Strains

AK-48	Jack the Ripper
American Dream	Jacky White
Artic Sun	Jilly Bean
Arjan's Haze #1	Kaya
Arjan's Haze #2	KC-36
Arjan's Haze #3	KC-45
Aurora Borealis	Kish
B-52	Kiwiskunk
BC Blueberry	Kushage
BC God Bud	LA Confidential
BC Sweet Tooth	Lowryder #2
Big Bang	Malawi Gold
Big Buddha Cheese	Martian Mean Green
Blue Buddha	Motavation
Blue Cheese	Mother's Finest
Brainstorm Haze	Mount Cook
Burmese Kush	Nuken
Chrystal	Opium
Cinderella 99x Panama Red	Posh
Ed Rosenthal Super Bud	Purple Kush
F-13	Sadhu
First Lady	Somaui
Fruit of the Gods	Somini
Fruity Thai	Sour Cream
Gonzo #1	Sour Diesel IBL
Grandaddy Grape Ape	Speed Queen
Grape Krush	Spoetnik #1
Hashberry	Sputnik
Haze Mist	Strawberry Haze
Ice Cream	Sweet 105
	The Church

The Doctor
The Purps
True Blue
Ultra Haze #1
Ultra Haze #2
Venus
Very Berry Haze
Wappa
White Berry
White Rhino
White Satin
White Smurf
Wonder Woman

Greenhouse Recommended Varieties

American Dream
Artic Sun
Aurora Borealis
Chrystal
Fruity Thai
Haze Mist
LA Confidential
Martina Mean Green
Sadhu
Sour Cream
Sour Diesel IBL
Sweet 105
Very Berry Haze
White Smurf

 Sea of Green Recommended Varieties

AK-48
American Dream
Aurora Borealis
B-52
BC God Bud
BC Sweet God
BC Sweet Tooth
Big Bang
Big Buddha Cheese
Blue Buddha
Blue Cheese
Burmese Kush
Chrystal
Cinderella 99x Panama Red
D-line (aka Chocolope)
Ed Rosenthal Super Bud
First Lady
Fruit of the Gods
Fruity Thai
Gonzo #1
Hashberry
Haze Mist
Ice Cream
Jack the Ripper
Jilly Bean
Kaya
KC-36
KC-45
Kish

Kiwiskunk
Kushage
LA Confidential
Lowryder #2
Martian Mean Green
Motavation
Mother's Finest
Mount Cook
Nuken
Opium
Posh
Purple Kush
Sadhu
Somini
Sour Cream
Sour Diesel IBL
Speed Queen
Spoetnik #1
The Purps
T.N.R.
Venus
Wappa
White Berry
White Rhino
White Satin
White Smurf
Wonder Woman

 **Feminized**

Arjan's Haze #2
Arjan's Haze #3 Ice Cream
Jacky White
Kaya
Opium
Spoetnik #1
Strawberry Haze
Sweet 105
The Church
The Doctor
Ultra Haze #1
Ultra Haze #2
Venus
Wappa
White Berry
Wonder Woman

Essays & Stories

Thanks to all of the businesses and organizations that supported this project.

The Big Book of **BUDS** volume 3

More Marijuana Varieties from the World's Great Seed Breeders

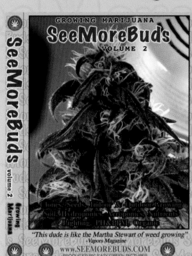

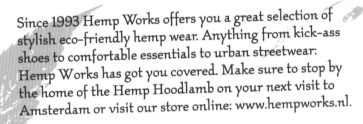

SKUNK
stinkin' it to the man
The Only Pot Mag You'll Ever Need!!!
• The Best Grow
• The Best News
• The Best Events
• The Best Photos
• The Best Writers
• The Best Products
• The Best Writers
• The Best...Period
www.skunkmagazine.com

CANNABIS SATIVA L.

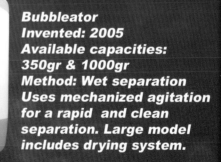

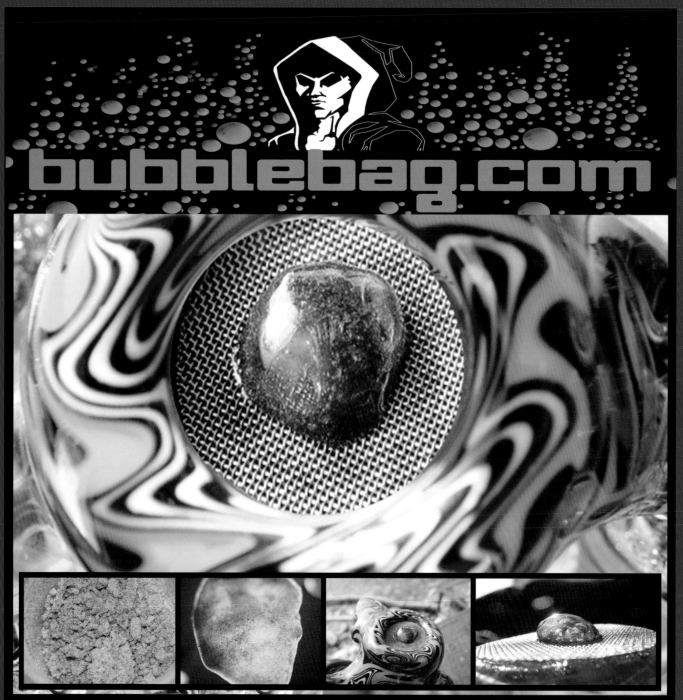

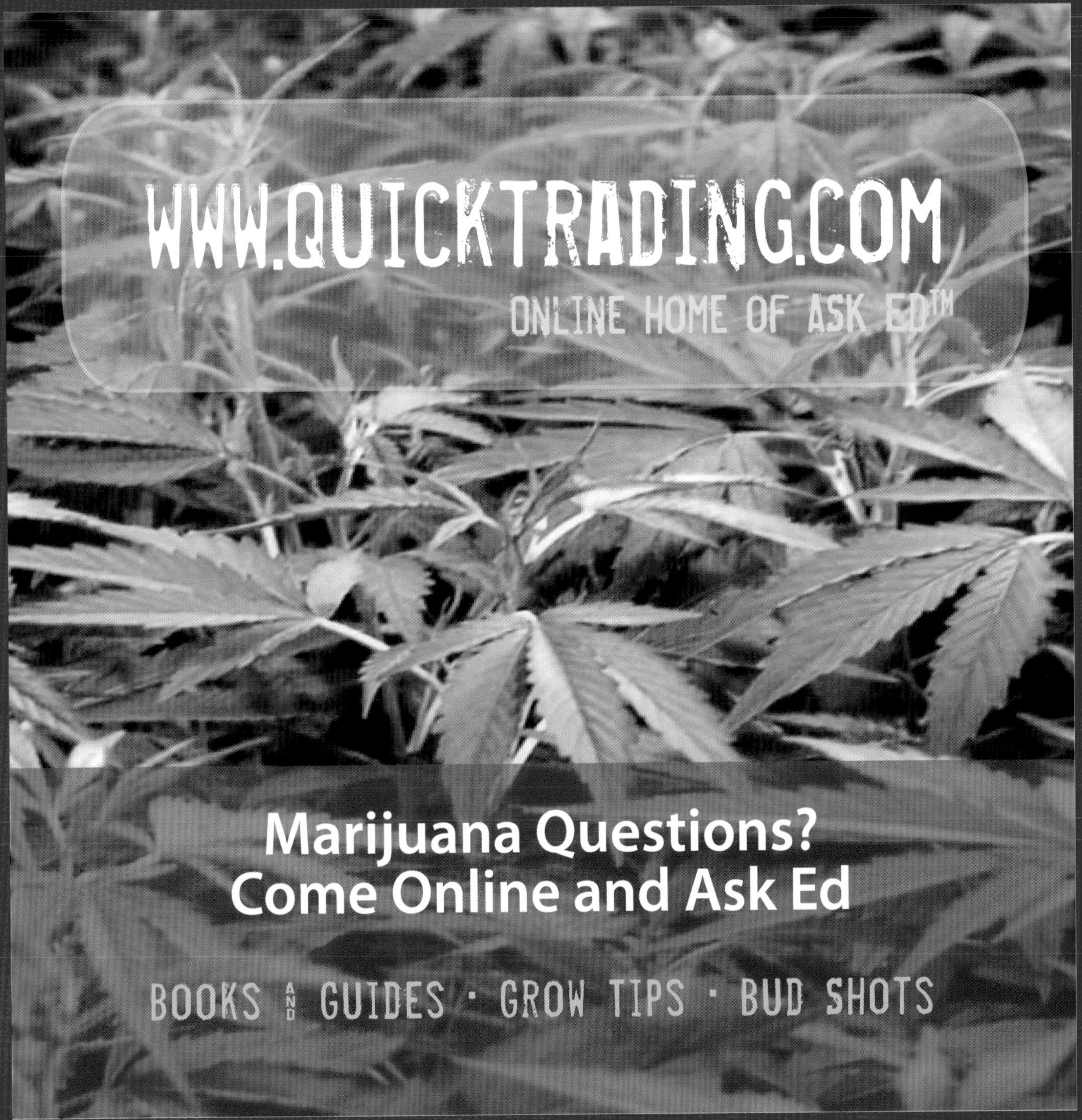
WWW.QUICKTRADING.COM
ONLINE HOME OF ASK ED™
Marijuana Questions?
Come Online and Ask Ed
BOOKS AND GUIDES · GROW TIPS · BUD SHOTS

Quick Key to Icons

English • En Español • Deutsch
En Français • Italiano • Nederlands

Strain Type

Sativa

Indica

Sativa/Indica

Indica/Sativa

Sativa/Ruderalis

Indica/Ruderalis

Feminized

Growing Info

Flowering time
Tiempo de floración
Blütezeit
Durée de floraison
Stagione della fioritura
Bloetijd

Parents
Genética
Mutterpflanze
Descendance
Genitori
Stamboom

Yield
Rendimiento
Ertag
Rendement
Raccolta
Opbrengst

SOG

Sea of Green

Indoor
Interior
Drinnen
d'Intérieur
Dentro
Binnen

Outdoor
Exterior
Draussen
d'Extérieur
Fuori
Buiten

Indoor/Outdoor
Interior/Exterior
Drinnen/Draussen
d'Intérieur/d'Extérieur
Dentro/Fuori
Binnen/Buiten

Sensory Experience

Buzz
Efecto
die Art des Turns
Effets
Effetti
High Effekt

Taste/Smell
Sabor/Aroma
Geschmack/Geruch
Saveur/Arôme
Sapore/Odore
Smaak/Geua

Breeder Location

Australia

Canada

Netherlands

Spain

United Kingdom

U.S.A.

Notes

A-Train • Afropips First Grade Malawi Go
Arjans Haze #1 • Arjans Haze #2 • A
BC Blueberry • BC God Bud • BC Swee
Blue Buddha • Blue Cheese • Brainstor
Chrystal • Cinderella 99 x Panama Red •
First Lady • Fruit of the Gods • Fruity Tha
Grape Ape • Grape Krush • Hashberry
Jack the Ripper • Jacky White • Jilly
Kiwiskunk • Kushage • LA Confidential • L
Green • Motavation • Mothers Finest •
Purple Kush • Sadhu • Somaui • Somini
Queen • Spoetnik #1 • Sputnik • (Arjar
Church • The Doctor • The Purps • T
(Arjans) Ultra Haze #1 • (Arjans) Ultra
Wappa • White Berry • White Smurf • Wh